The Legend of

MOLLY BOLIN

Women's Pro Basketball Trailblazer

STEPHEN H. PROVOST

Dragon Crown Books 2019
All rights reserved.

ISBN: 1-949971-01-5
ISBN-13: 978-1-949971-01-9

Dedication

This book is dedicated to all my fellow pioneers of the first Women's Professional Basketball League, the WBL, who played for the love of the game and believed we deserved a future in this sport. It is past time for your courage, dedication and determination to recognized: You helped break down barriers for all women in professional basketball. I am humbled and grateful to have played a part in this history. There would not be a present without a past.

Molly Bolin Kazmer
March 12, 2019

Contents

Acknowledgements

First and foremost, I'm grateful to Molly Kazmer for the extensive information, photos and feedback she contributed to this project. This was truly a collaborative venture. Without Molly's consistent input and commitment to this project from start to finish, it would not have been possible. I'd also like to extend my thanks to Molly's former teammates, coaches, competitors and friends who provided information for this work. Among them: Dave Almstead, Tom Davis, Doris Draving, Bruce Mason, Tanya Crevier, Tony Mercurio, Robin Tucker, Greg Williams and Carolyn Woodward. Your contributions are greatly appreciated.

Foreword
by Greg Williams

"Machine Gun" Molly Bolin ... have you heard of her? No? Well, she may be the best female basketball player you have never heard of. I hope this book changes that lack of recognition.

I first became aware of Molly as an assistant coach with the Houston Angels of the first women's professional basketball league, the WBL. We became bitter rivals with her team, the Iowa Cornets, and would ultimately square off against each other in the first WBL Championship Finals, a grueling five-game series. Head coach Don Knodel and I knew our only chance to win was to somehow make "Machine Gun" Molly shoot a few blanks instead of the beautiful and deadly jump shot that had earned her the famous (and perfect) nickname she was known by to the fans and media alike.

Molly was one of those rare athletes who would make you sit on the edge of your seat (or hold your breath, if you were an opposing coach) every time she touched the ball. You could not help but think: What is she going to do next? She brought a flair and excitement to the too few fans who were fortunate enough to see her making incredible shots all over the court.

Having been a head coach in three women's professional leagues (WBL, WABA, WNBA), I think Molly's unique ability would have made her a star in today's game just as it did 40 years ago when she exploded on the unknowing basketball world. Jordan, Magic, Kobe, LeBron ... household names to basketball fans all over the world. "Machine Gun" Molly Bolin was literally a "shooting star" who, unfortunately, burned just a little before her time. But, thank goodness, times have changed in women's basketball with Title IX, the NCAA, and the WNBA celebrating 20 years of competition.

So, who is "Machine Gun" Molly Bolin? She is a true women's basketball pioneer who made her own way through new and unknown hoop history, constantly moving and probing the defense to make a small mistake so she could unleash her high-arcing jump shots and drives to the basket and get the "and-1."

Now sit back, relax and imagine that beautiful and unforgettable sound like a "Machine Gun" Molly Bolin jump shot: "SWISH ... Nothin' but Net."

Introduction

Throughout my career as an author and journalist, I've been fascinated by stories that, for one reason or another, have been forgotten or overlooked. The desire to hear and preserve such stories led me to write books about the history of my hometown, old highways, department stores and defunct sports leagues.

The last of these, *A Whole Different League*, turned out to be a stepping-stone to this work. If you look at the cover, you'll see Molly Bolin's photo at the upper right. Before I wrote that book, I didn't know who she was. But when I learned about her achievements on the court, I was amazed I'd her name didn't ring a bell. Somehow, I'd spent 10 years as a sportswriter and editor and had never once heard of Molly Bolin.

Yes, she played in the Women's Basketball League, which itself has been largely forgotten. When I was researching *A Whole Different League*, the chapter on the WBL was the last one I wrote. It seems I had forgotten about it, too. But this was no second-rate league; it was a true counterpart to the NBA at a time when women's athletics were coming into their own (thanks to Title IX) and women's basketball had just become an

Olympic sport.

During its three years of existence, the WBL featured all-time greats like Ann Meyers, Carol Blazejowski and Nancy Lieberman, each a familiar name to me and each a Hall of Famer. But here's the kicker: Molly scored more points than any of them. In fact, as of this writing, she *still* holds women's pro basketball records for:

- Most points in a game.
- Most points in a season.
- Highest scoring average in a season.
- Most field goals in a season.
- Most points in a playoff game.

Each of these records has stood for 40 years, through more than 20 seasons of the WNBA. But Molly was making history even before she joined the WBL. She once scored 83 points in a high school game and was the first woman to sign a with a women's pro basketball league when he joined the Iowa Cornets in 1978. Her 55, 54 and 53 points in WBL contests rank first, second and tied for third all-time among the pros, and she was an all-star in each of her three seasons.

Her warm-up gear is on display at the Naismith Hall of Fame in Springfield, Mass. Yet somehow, inexplicably, hasn't been inducted into the Women's Basketball Hall of Fame as an individual. This seems like keeping Babe Ruth out of Cooperstown ... except that many of the Bambino's records have been broken, while most of Molly's still stand. Babe's iconic single-season home run record of 60 proved less durable than the scoring standards Molly set: It stood for 34 years.

Molly's credentials are impressive, to say the least. But don't take my word for it: Linda Thompson Jenner of NBC's *SportsWorld* called Molly "the purest shooter to play women's basketball."

Greg Williams knows the game as well as anyone. The only coach to lead women's teams in three pro leagues, he's also coached Division I basketball at Rice and women's hoops at Houston and Colorado State. He had this to say about Molly: "She's one of the very few female or even male basketball players that, when she got the ball, you were always on the edge of your seat. She just had such a charisma about her. You just never knew what she was going to do when she got the ball, other than she was going to score two points."

Donna Geils Orender, who played against Molly for three seasons in the WBL and later served as president of the WNBA, told Slam Magazine in 2013: "She didn't look like an athlete per se, but she'd score from everywhere on the floor. She was unbelievable."

Iowa Cornets owner George Nissen called her scoring "uncanny," and Cornets coach Dan Moulton declared she was "the best out-shooter in the league."

When I was writing *A Whole Different League*, I reached out to Molly for her recollections of the WBL and realized her story fill a book all on its own. By happy coincidence, it was a story she'd been wanting to share.

It's the story of Iowa's 6-on-6 girls basketball phenomenon, of a shooting stroke that's evoked comparisons to Stephen Curry and earned her the nickname "Machine Gun Molly"; of a poster that made Molly the sports world's answer to Farrah Fawcett; and of a league that paved the way for the WNBA.

But most of all, it's the story of an athlete who overcame the odds time and again through hard work and dedication. It's a story of a young girl from a small town in Iowa who had a dream, pursued it and made it come true. It's exactly the kind of story I love to tell, and I'm pleased to present it here.

Stephen H. Provost

Stephen H. Provost

Molly is depicted shooting, at left, on a mural in Moravia.

Homegrown Talent

A record crowd turned out in Cedar Rapids, Iowa, to see their team play one of its archrivals — and try to clinch a playoff spot.

The 5,386 fans at Five Seasons Center sensed that the Iowa Cornets, playing their second season in the Women's Basketball League, were poised to make another run at the championship. They'd fallen just short in their inaugural season, losing to Houston in the finals, but they were enjoying another strong year with a 19-12 record, a single game behind the Minnesota Fillies at 18-9.

As fate would have it, Minnesota was the team standing between the Cornets and a playoff spot on March 2, 1980.

But the fans weren't worried. On the contrary, the arena was abuzz with anticipation. The Fillies might have been ahead of them in the standings, but the Cornets had their kryptonite.

Her name was Molly Bolin.

Molly didn't just have the Fillies' number, she was in the middle of a historic season in which she would average a record 32.8 points a game. But she seemed to be even hotter against the Fillies. She'd set a league record with 53 points against Minnesota a year earlier — only to go herself one better with 54 less than two months ago. That game was also against the Fillies, who proved to be no match for the Cornets in a 109-93 blowout.

With Molly in the lineup, there was simply no way the Cornets were going to lose to the Fillies.

And Molly was in the lineup ... at least in the beginning.

She led the Cornets out to a fast start, and she got a standing ovation at the end of the first quarter when news came out over the public address system that she'd just scored her 1,000[th] point for the season, something no one else had ever done. The Cornets took a 29-18 lead as the quarter ended and appeared poised to blow the visitors out as the second period began. But then, the unthinkable happened. Just 42 seconds into the period, Molly collided with another player and went crashing to the floor. Hard.

It was her left shoulder, the one she'd injured in a childhood game of one-on-one with a neighbor boy: a rotator cuff injury that she'd never had fixed. She'd landed on her elbow, pushing the shoulder out of its socket, and she was in extreme pain.

"Even though I had accidentally put my shoulder out of place before — just a few times since the original rotator cuff injury — this was the first time it happened on the court in my pro career, and the timing couldn't have been worse."

Coach Steve Kirk summed it up succinctly after the game: "If she can't play," he said, "we aren't going anyplace."

As she lay there on her back, Tanya Crevier, a teammate

who was doubling as team trainer, ran out onto the floor, but she knew immediately she was out of her element and went looking for a doctor.

But Molly took matters into her own hands: Focusing through the pain, she tried to relax her shoulder and pull her arm down to get it back in place: "I was not going to miss this big game, and I certainly wasn't going to wait for someone else to fix it."

After about 5 minutes, she got her shoulder in its socket again and found her way to the bench.

She didn't stay there long. Before the second quarter was even halfway over, she told Kirk she wanted to go back in. Had Cornets been blessed with a proper medical staff, she probably wouldn't have been allowed back on the court. But even if a doctor had been there, she says, "I wasn't going to let anyone tell me to sit out."

So, she went back out and not only picked up where she left off, she turned her game up a notch. The Cornets outscored the Fillies 35-17 in the second quarter for a 64-35 halftime lead and never looked back. By the time it was over, Molly had broken her own single-game record yet again with 55 points, hitting 22 of her 34 shots from the field and 11 of 12 free throws. The Cornets led by as many as 45 points en route to a 125-85 blowout of Minnesota.

Life in Moravia

It wouldn't be the last time Molly scored 50 points in a single game. In fact, she would torch the Fillies yet again in the playoffs, scoring 50 — including 32 in the first half — as they routed Minnesota 128-111 in Cedar Rapids. It was almost second nature to her by that point. In fact, she had scored 50 or more so often during high school that she *averaged* nearly 55 a game for the Moravia High Mohawkettes, once pouring in as many as 83 in a game. (And those games were just 32 minutes long, compared to 48 minutes in the pros.)

But her phenomenal shooting is just part of Molly's story.

It's a story that began with a young girl playing basketball in the snow in Moravia, Iowa. It continues today as Molly works to bring recognition to the WBL as the crucible of women's pro basketball in the United States, a brave endeavor that helped pave the way for a slew of Olympic medals and the success of the WNBA.

Molly, age 5

It started on Friday the 13th — at least that's what she thought for many years. It turns out, however, that she was born on a Wednesday (Nov. 13) in Dryden, Ontario, Canada, where her father was working on a pipeline job. Molly isn't her given name. It's actually Monna, the third in a line of rhyming sister names, following Donna and Jonna — four and five years older, respectively. But when Donna acquired the nickname "Dolly," her younger sisters became "Jolly" and "Molly."

The only one of six children to be born outside the country, she moved with her family to Phoenix, where she skipped kindergarten and entered first grade at the age of 5. Then, in 1965, they traveled to Iowa — her parents' home state — to take care of her grandfather in New Sharon. Her parents, Forrest and Wanda Van Benthuysen, had intended to move back to

Phoenix, but they lost the house there and wound up staying in New Sharon.

There were just six of them by this point: Older siblings Marvin and Sally, 12 and 10 years older than Molly, respectively, stayed behind in Arizona. Dolly, Jolly, Molly and the youngest, Forrest, joined their parents in New Sharon and, three years later, when they moved about an hour south to Moravia. Molly's father had gotten a job there building Rathbun Dam, creating a reservoir that supplies water to nearly 16,000 farms and rural families in the region.

Just before the start of Molly's fifth-grade year, the family moved into a trailer next to the rail line and not far from the elementary school. Later, they would move into a small house about two or three miles from town, across from a church and cemetery.

Not much has changed in Moravia over the years. The population has held steady between around 600 or 700 people ever since the turn of the 20th century. It's still much the same, in many ways, as it was when Molly was growing up there: One of the three small grocery stores that served the town is still open, and most of the original brick buildings are still standing. The small community building with the library, where Molly spent many of her Saturdays, is still there on the town square, where a water tower emblazoned with the town's name stood sentinel.

Even though Moravia was more than a century old by the time Molly arrived, its roads weren't paved when she was growing up there.

The town had three grocery stores, but getting any food other than the basics (milk, bread, sugar and flour) was a treat in the Van Benthuysen household. Molly's father would bring home fish he'd caught or game, but everything else was homegrown. There was a big garden with fruit trees and vegetables that Molly's mother canned, which were kept in a "dank, nasty basement" until the family was ready for them. ("We ate a lot of good non-GMO foods and had zero appreciation for it!" she says now.)

Molly's mom also raised chickens, which were served for dinner, too — over the objections of Molly and her younger brother, Forrest.

It wasn't always clear which chicken play the unfortunate role of entrée.

"My brother and I would befriend the chickens and cry and refuse to eat them when their number came up and they were served for dinner," she says. "My mom hated killing the chickens but kept a row of 16-ounce pop bottles outside the door; when the chickens got into our garden, she would come out throwing them and usually hit one that we had to eat for dinner."

You could find white-tailed deer, Canada geese and wild turkey around the area. And raccoons. Molly loved the raccoons.

"My parents made all of us work on my aunt's pig farm in Knoxville," a town about the size of Moravia about an hour to the north, "to earn money for school clothes," she says. "While I was there once, I rescued a baby raccoon that I raised, and I was hooked from then on: I rescued and raised several raccoons and even took one to my college dorm and fed with an eyedropper every three hours to keep him alive. I *loved* baby raccoons and collected 'raccoon everything' until I finally got over it. I once drove from Iowa to California with a raccoon in my backseat!"

Apart from rescuing raccoons and riding ponies, which she borrowed from people in the area, leisure activities were hard to come by. Molly taught herself to play the piano by ear, but she had to be inventive just to pass the time.

"As you would think in a small town, I spent a lot of time riding my bike around trying to find something to do, as there wasn't much," she says. "We only had one TV station, so were bored out of our minds out there in the middle of nowhere when we lived in the country. We would play board games for hours, and I would explore behind the house, where there was a pond and try to catch snakes and bullfrogs. I would go over to the cemetery and read all the headstones and play the piano for hours inside the little church."

There was also a skating rink on the edge of town — but it cost 50 cents she usually didn't have in her pocket, and it was only open once or twice a week, anyway.

Then there was the Moravia Fall Festival each September, with carnival rides, tents, parades, and tents for the contests for things like produce and artwork.

"I would ride my bike up to the square to watch the tents go up and get excited about the carnival," she recalls. "My dog had puppies when we first moved to Moravia, so my little brother and I entered the kiddie parade dressed as dog catchers with the puppies in a wagon and won first prize. This was such a big deal, and we were so thrilled to win a few ride tickets."

Struggle and opportunity

Life at home could be difficult. Money was tight, and Molly learned to work hard for what she wanted. Her father's work was seasonal and sporadic, and "he managed what money he had poorly."

He also had a problem with alcohol: "After moving back to Iowa and Moravia, my dad was in a bad truck accident and had a real drinking problem. When he was building our house by a main road, he would pass out from drinking and be seen by anyone driving by. In a small town of 700 people, there was a stigma that went with that — of being like 'trailer trash' or something. My mom was mortified about it, and her feeling that way rubbed off on me."

The alcohol took its toll on the family, and Molly's father was abusive to her mother. One time, she had enough and stood her ground, and challenged him that the next time he would never see her or us again. He must have believed her, because the physical abuse stopped.

"But nobody — law or social services — ever did anything to protect her, so she stood her ground and was very strong and resilient and survived some tough times, which has been a theme for females in my family," she says. "I think the one time she had enough and stood her ground and challenged him to just do it. He never threatened her again."

Life at school was much better. Molly was recognized on Feb. 15, 1968, in the *Moravia Union* — among the first of many times her name would appear in print — for perfect attendance during the first semester. She didn't pull straight A's, but she was a better-than-average student, and she had friends but wasn't the center of attention socially.

"I grew up with friends but not necessarily 'popular,' and I definitely had some self-esteem issues because of not having money," she recalls. "I was a good student — mostly B's — and was involved in anything and everything that would get me out of the house, from sports, to clubs, to theatre and music."

Molly played clarinet, was involved in the local 4-H Club and took weekly baton-twirling lessons, at just 10 cents apiece. It was a small price to pay, especially considering the door those lessons opened for her.

It was the door at the local gym, site of a local high school basketball game.

What she saw when she passed through that door changed her life.

'I've got to do this'

"I've always had sort of a thing that I never wanted to miss out on anything going on around me," she says, and there was plenty going on inside the gym: "Everyone in town was there because there was nothing else to do. The place was packed, the band was playing and they were selling popcorn. I walked into that gym and I thought, 'I've got to do this. This is the coolest thing I've ever seen in my life.'"

Soon, she *was* doing it, whenever she got the chance, even in the winter and even if it was snowing out.

Molly's neighbor, Carolyn Woodward, recalls, "She played basketball even with snow on the ground in the winter. She'd shovel out the place just to play basketball. She practiced a lot — that's what made her such a good player."

"In Iowa, there was always snow on the ground during basketball season," Molly explains. "You're in a heavy coat, and you're playing on a bent rim with no backboard."

She wasn't alone in her enthusiasm for basketball — at least, not among girls in Iowa, where the game was popular. Outside the state, though, it was a different story. On a summer trip to visit her older sister, an air-traffic controller in Lincoln, Nebraska, she recalled surprising everyone when she took on all comers and beat five different boys in a series of one-on-one games.

Back home, she started playing one-on-one against boys from around the neighborhood. A couple of neighbors across the street had basketball hoops, and she played there when she could, although more often than not, their cars were parked in the driveway. "Thinking back, I must have really bugged them in those days," she says, "but I know they realized it paid off"

More often, she'd practice next door.

"The junior high coach was my next-door neighbor, and most of the one-on-one battles in the snow took place in his driveway with a bent hoop with no net," she says. "I'm not sure why, but I only played against boys off the court. There were no girls around who wanted to play outside as much as I did."

From middle school onward, she says, most of her social interaction during the day took place on outdoor basketball courts: "When my dad traveled for summer jobs, I would take my ball and find an outdoor court to play on and usually stay for hours until dark.

"I think most of the top players from my era learned basketball this way and were sometimes called 'street players' in learning aggressive, sometimes dirty style of play. One of the best compliments a girl could get in those days is 'You play like a guy!' However, that was not me. Learning fundamentals at camp and playing the Iowa girls rules, I wanted to play like a girl and still beat the guys. Never being a physical player, I had to use quickness and finesse to compete and throw a lot of fakes to put the defense off balance when they were trying to block my shot. Most of the time it worked well up to a point where the male skill level/size was out of my league."

Often, she wound up playing one particular neighbor boy. They were fairly evenly matched, but he could be a sore loser when she got the better of him: "If I beat him, he threw the ball as hard as he could down the street and went home. I had to go get it."

She also wound up playing against the boy's younger brother, who could be even more temperamental.

"I liked to play against the older one, but the younger one was a hothead," she says. "He twisted my arm behind my back."

When he did, she suffered the rotator cuff injury that she aggravated during her record 55-point game against the Minnesota Fillies. But that didn't stop her from playing — not as a teenager, and not ever.

Molly in her back yard, with the church cemetery in the background

Stephen H. Provost

Molly, third row-center, attends the Parsons College basketball camp.

Moravia's Shooting Star

A small item appeared in the December 17, 1970, edition of the *Moravia Union*, about two-thirds of the way down the page in the far-right column. "Junior High Teams Win Two At Moulton," the headline announced. The girls team came away with a 20-14 victory. The high scorer, with 13 points, was Molly Van Benthuysen.

Naturally.

Not long after her first visit to a high school game, Molly had begun playing basketball herself, but she had to wait a couple of years before joining an organized team because the elementary school didn't have one. There was, however, a "Family Fun Night" that featured a couple of games: One matched the high school girls team against their male teachers (dressed as girls!), while the other pitted teams of fifth- and sixth-grade students against each other.

"I started going to the playground on my own to practice

for the big game on Family Fun Night — and we won both years," she recalls.

Molly's junior high team played an eight-game season, with four games at home and four on the road. The girls practiced in an old building at the elementary school and played Saturday mornings in the high school gym.

Meanwhile, she continued her baton-twirling and won a competition that landed her live appearance on TV right after one of her Saturday games.

As 1971 got under way, she poured in 23 points — more than the entire opposing team combined — in a 41-20 homecourt victory over Russell. It was a familiar theme for Molly's eighth-grade season: She finished the year averaging 16.3 points a game, scoring a school-record 25 points in one, as her team lost just one of its eight starts.

Summer camps

The next time her name appeared in the paper, it was in an announcement that she had attended a July basketball camp at Parsons College in Fairfield, about an hour east of Moravia. There, she was a member of the camp's championship team, was named the player with the most improved set shot, and placed among the top five in the both the "lane drill" and the "Mikan drill," the *Union* reported.

"All the drills were timed," Molly says. "Everything we did was a contest, from free throws to dribbling figure-8s, with awards given away to the top five in each category. As there were over 100 girls there, I made sure I went home winning at least four or five awards."

Among her favorites was the Mikan drill, named after legendary big man George Mikan of the Minneapolis Lakers. Molly describes it as "shooting a right-hand layup with one step, catching the ball — hopefully from the net — and one step across and shooting a left-hand layup: as many as you could do in 30 seconds."

"This is a drill I practiced extensively on my own until I was dizzy, on outdoor baskets," she says.

Sometimes, it would be after dark before she finished, because she wouldn't stop practicing until she made 10 in a row.

The Fairfield camp was run by Bob Spencer, head basketball coach at Parsons College, who would go on to coach for several years at William Penn before spending more than a decade as women's basketball coach at

Parsons College girls basketball camp, July 30, 1972

Fresno State. In 27 years as a head coach, his teams won 578 games and compiled a winning percentage of .681, so it's no surprise that Molly counts him as her most influential coach.

"He was way ahead of the times, running a weeklong, live-in camps with hundreds of players attending over eight or nine summer sessions," she says. "It was very disciplined both on and off the court, and I heard numerous stories on how other high school players I admired put the time in to become great. I believe that's also where I learned importance of setting goals, which I did every year I played."

Molly's first goal was just getting to the camp, which proved to be a challenge. Her eighth-grade coach had recommended it as a way to improve her shooting. But since her family didn't have much money, and camp tuition was $75, Molly had to raise the necessary cash herself.

It wasn't as though her parents would have helped, anyway: At the beginning, they weren't too keen on supporting her dream of succeeding at basketball.

"Athletics were not a focus for my family," she remembers, although siblings Dolly and Forrest played basketball at Moravia, too, and Jolly was a cheerleader. "My dad considered sport to be hunting and fishing, and my parents were totally not on board with it. When I didn't do the dishes once, my mom tried to keep me home from basketball practice as punishment. I said, 'Mom, that isn't going to work.'"

With her parents unable to help with the camp tuition, 13-year-old Molly had to get creative.

"I saw a card in a magazine and sent it in to get a greeting card kit — including Christmas cards — and I went door to door all over Moravia, telling them I was earning my way to basketball camp," she says. "These items were 50 cents to a dollar, with very few things costing more, so my profits were not very large."

After spending two months knocking on nearly every door in town, she had earned enough to cover the $25 deposit but was still $50 short of the total cost. Spencer, however, was impressed with her attitude and allowed her to work off the balance by serving in the food line during camp, where she spent the last two weeks of July.

She got her money's worth. A typical day started with breakfast at 7 a.m., followed by a half-hour of individual instruction. Drills, chalk talks and critiques continued throughout the day, with breaks at 11:30 for lunch and 6 p.m. for dinner, but that wasn't the end of it. After dinner came more instruction, followed by scrimmages and actual games from 7:30 to 9 p.m. Then came an hour of leisure time before lights out at 10 o'clock.

"It was a really intense camp," Molly remembers. "By the second or third day, you were peeling blisters off your feet."

But even that wasn't enough for Molly, who soaked it all in and still wanted more: "I asked for extra help before and after the sessions were over. I bought in completely to the program and put in my best efforts to learn and try hard. It was the first time I was learning fundamentals, and I was determined to be a good player, so I practiced what I was taught.

"Camp director Bob Spencer was so impressed with my work ethic he met with me privately and asked if I would like to come back to camp the following week for free. Of course, I jumped at the chance to stay another week and still worked the food line, blisters and all!"

Molly returned to the camp the following week and the year after that, when Spencer moved from Parsons College to William Penn University in Oskaloosa — and moved the camp there with him. It was only about half as far away as Fairfield, which made it more convenient for Molly, who by this time was earning her tuition by charging an hourly rate of 50 cents for babysitting and by detasseling corn for $1.40 an hour.

She also attended the Camp of Champs, directed by Bud McLearn, the highly respected coach of Mediapolis, that summer. Mediapolis High School had just won the state title, led by Deb Coates, then a sophomore like Molly.

"I remember having a bit of idol worship of her, since she was highly celebrated in the media and I watched her play in the state tournament on TV," Molly says, "and here I was competing with her at camp. Needless to say, I brought my A-game every day. I ended up winning Forward of the Week in that huge camp, as well a few other awards. That experience made me realize that I could compete at that level."

Freshman year

By that time, Molly was starting for the Moravia High team, but she hadn't been in the lineup at the outset. During her first year, the coach used a seniority system that kept freshmen on the bench — much as freshman were kept off the basketball court (and the football field) at NCAA universities before 1972.

At least Molly got some time off the bench, just not right away.

She got off on the wrong foot when she barely missed curfew the night before Moravia's first varsity game. She'd invited a boy to the school's Sadie Hawkins dance, and his parents had been late picking him up afterward. She waited until they arrived, then had to walk home and, by the time she got there, the curfew had passed. When her coach asked her the next day, she was honest.

"He pulled my uniform, which was the only time in my entire career I did not play," she says. "Being 14, I certainly did not understand the consequences."

Relegated to the junior varsity, Molly and her teammates there wore skirts the varsity team had worn the previous year — before converting to shorts.

"The JV team my ninth-grade year got the varsity skirts handed down, and they had red satin pants under the skirt as part of uniform," she says. "It was a disaster to forget to bring them to an away game! But since I had grown up seeing this uniform at the time, I loved wearing it. I remember playing in gyms so small the out-of-bounds line was just a few inches from the wall. A lot of those older small schools with the tiny gyms closed down and consolidated with other towns about that time. With the varsity we always played in pretty good-sized gyms, though."

In early December of 1971, Molly reeled off 48 points in a 75-73 junior varsity win over Blakesburg. A week later, she came through with a double-double (30 points and 10 rebounds) as the team improved its record to 6-1 with a Monday night victory at Moulton. Then, the following night, she was back on the varsity, scoring six points in a 91-37 rout of Mormon Trail.

The leading scorer in that game was a girl by the name of Fonda Dicks. No, that's not a misprint. That really *was* her name. (Comedian Tom Arnold, who grew up in nearby Ottumwa about the same time, would use it as material in a Twitter post 40 years later.) Fonda was ahead of Molly on the depth chart, and she was also the No. 1 scorer on the team. Against Mormon trail, she scored 45, and in another game, she set a school record with 69.

"She had an amazing jump shot, and I wanted to be just like her, so I was always feeding her the ball," Molly says.

But Molly was taking her own shots, too — and hitting them. During one game in December, she scored 27 points to lead all scorers (Dicks had 24). Even more impressive, she did so "wearing a cheerleader's tennis shoes, because I forgot and left mine at home."

6 on 6

Texas was football country. Indiana was the heartland of men's college basketball. And, in the same way, Iowa was the center of the universe for high school girls hoops.

In the Hawkeye State, the girls' game was more popular than the boys', and it had been for as long as anyone could remember. But it wasn't just your typical game of basketball; it was a 6-on-6 game that had been created to be less strenuous on the (supposedly) more fragile female athlete.

Players like Molly blew such assumptions out of the water, and they'd been doing so for years by the time she came along. Sandra Fiete poured in more than 4,800 points by the time she graduated from Garnavillo in 1955. At Mediapolis, Deb Coates scored more than 5,100 points in a career that ran from 1971 to '75. Denise Long, who attended Union-Whitten High School a couple of hours north of Moravia, set a career scoring record of 6,250 points in 1969 that would stand for two decades — not just for Iowa, but for the entire nation. She once scored 111 points in a game and averaged an astonishing 68.5 points as a senior.

Players could average more than 50 points because the action was so fast-paced, and because only three of the six payers on the court at any one time were eligible to score. Molly was one of three forwards for the Moravia High School Mohawkettes; three other players were designated as guards. But those positions weren't the same as in a standard 5-on-5 game.

The three forwards spent the entire game in the front court; they were the only ones who ever took a shot. The guards, meanwhile, stayed in the backcourt, playing nothing but defense.

After the ball went through the basket on one end, the referee would grab it and throw it to the other team at halfcourt. Forwards would only play defense after a missed shot or a free throw, and players were only allowed to dribble the ball twice before passing.

Molly once scored 83 points in a game for Moravia High School. Here, she shows off her vertical leap.

The game became a sensation because it was so much fun to watch. In Moravia, fans would make sure to be in their seats by the time the girls tipped off, usually as the first half of a doubleheader with the boys.

"In a big role-reversal, if our boys had a losing record, a lot of people would leave after the girls game or go home by halftime of the boys game," Molly recalls. "It was such a high-scoring game. We went from offense to offense, scoring to scoring, and that's what made it so popular."

The girls at Moravia High even got equal time to use the gym for practice.

"We alternated the use of the gym with the boys, with practice right after school every other day and late practice alternate days starting at 5:30 p.m. I don't know of anywhere else in the country in the '70s that female basketball players got equal gym time or equal game billing with the boys."

The team got plenty of media attention, as well. The *Moravia Union* carried news of the team's games on its front page, and newspapers across the state covered the Mohawkettes, who competed in the eight-team Bluegrass Conference along with other high schools in the area: Wayne, Southeast Warren, Lamoni, Seymour, Leon, Mormon Trail and Melcher-Dallas.

Moravia hadn't suffered through a losing season since 1959, an impressive feat for a small school in an era before Iowa placed similarly sized high schools in the same division.

There were just a dozen girls in Molly's class.

"The girls team had a long tradition of being winners, which raised the expectations of the coach, players and entire community who expected this tradition to continue," she says. "The games were covered extensively by the press, not only in Moravia's once-weekly paper, but most of the surrounding community newspapers, including the Ottumwa Courier, which was the largest, covering all the smaller communities within a radius."

Varsity starter

During Molly's first two years of high school, she played a supporting role to Fonda. But with Molly moving up to the varsity squad full time during her sophomore year, she started to narrow the gap between them. In a 103-90 loss against Colfax in January 1973, Fonda led the way with 51 points, but Molly had 32 of her own. Together, they accounted for 83 of the team's 90 points. Fonda might have been queen of the court at Moravia, but Molly was setting herself up as the heir apparent.

Off the court, Molly was involved in just about every activity you could think of at Moravia High.

"Other than sports, I was in marching band, I was a twirler

for two years and drum majorette two years, and we marched in parades and competitions as well as halftime of all home football games," she says. "There was a lot of time put in practice, but it was almost always in the fall prior to basketball, and I juggled it with softball. I played clarinet in grade school but loved the baton better."

Molly was also involved in nearly every club the school had to offer at one time another during her four years at MHS, ranging from Future Homemakers of America (her comment looking back: "Yuck!") to Spanish Club; from Science Club and Pep Club to Future Teachers of American and a year on the yearbook staff.

"My sophomore year I think was the most fun I had other than being a senior," she says. "Besides marching band, I was in the musical *Bye Bye Birdie* as one of the teenage girls, and there were just a lot of fun times."

In fact, she appeared in every school play and musical once or twice a year, and was in the school's Swing Choir, which traveled for performances and competitions. She enjoyed that a lot ... until the choir director decided to schedule performances the summer before her senior year, when she had plans to attend basketball camp.

She chose basketball (of course) and got kicked out of the choir.

Basketball itself, however, wasn't without conflict. Molly's sophomore season was marred by dissention on the team, as all the seniors got together and wrote a letter to the school board in the hopes of getting coach Keith Markow fired. But Molly, who was close friends with the coach's daughter, found herself caught in the middle. She didn't sign the letter and didn't take sides in the dispute; the coach wound up keeping his job — at least until the end of the season.

Even amid that friction, the team was nearly unstoppable ... except against Colfax, which denied the Mohawkettes a spot in the state tournament by beating them 86-83 for the regional title. Fonda finished the game with 42 points, and Molly had 23 as Moravia finished the season with just three losses in 28 games — two of them to Colfax. Fonda wound up as selected to the all-state first team, while Molly received honorable mention after averaging 20.9 points a game.

"I was so sure that this was the year I would play in the state tournament, it was a painful blow to be eliminated," Molly says. "However, once the sting of the loss subsided a bit, I went right back to working on her game on the playgrounds until summer camp."

The effort was about to pay off, even if the press was skeptical. The team had a new coach, and Molly was the only returning starter, so expectations were low. Molly, however, was intent on proving those expectations wrong: "I was about as hyped as possible to step on the court again."

When she did, in the 1973-74 season opener Nov. 13 against Centerville the results surpassed everyone's expectations — even her own. She celebrated her 16th birthday by scoring an astonishing 63 points — just six shy of Fonda Dicks' school record and nearly three-quarters of Moravia's total — in an 85-73 win.

It was a major achievement, but she wasn't about to rest on her laurels.

She recalls thinking to herself, "Now that I know what I can do, I'm not going back." After that, she says, "I was really hard on myself if I didn't score 50 or 60 points. We had games where four or six players were out with the flu, but I said, 'Hell, no. We're not going to lose!'"

On Dec. 4, she exploded for 70 points in a 92-74 win over

Lamoni, besting Dicks' school record by a single point.

James Schnack, who had replaced Markow as the Mohawketts' head coach, described her as "a good driver and a good outside shooter" who was "tough to stop in a one-on-one situation" and "tremendously quick."

As Christmas approached, Molly was tied for the state's scoring lead with Deb Coates of Mediapolis. Each has scored 268 points so far for a 53.6 average, and each had a high game of 70. Molly dropped to third on the list the following week at 52.1 points a game, even though she scored 55 and 42 points in a pair of outings while playing with a sprained ankle. A few weeks later, she poured in 65 points — including 31 in the fourth quarter — to lead Moravia past Wayne 82-68, and she matched that total during an 81-52 rout of Centerville in the sectional final, outscoring the Redettes all by herself.

She finished the season as the state's third-leading scorer, but had to settle for second-team all-state honors even though two of the players on the first team wound up behind her on the list. (Connie Kunzmann of Everly, a future teammate with the Cornets, was a third-team choice as a senior that year.)

The team barely missed the state tournament, finishing Molly's junior year with a 20-5 record and placing third in the district tournament after a heartbreaking 85-84 loss to Wayne. Molly scored 64 points in the game, but Moravia lost when Wayne's Rhonda Cobb capped a 40-point game by nailing a 22-foot jumper with 3 seconds left.

Molly soon turned her attention to her senior season. Basketball was her primary sport, but she stayed in shape by playing shortstop on the softball team and competing for the track team in the hurdles, high jump and relays. "If you wanted to stay in shape," she says, "you had to do the other sports."

Track helped keep her legs strong: She developed a vertical

leap once measured at 30 inches that enabled her to shoot over taller defenders on the court. She qualified for the state track meet as a freshman and sophomore, once in the relays and once in the high hurdles, where she set school and conference records in the 100 and 220.

But she hated distance running — "especially in freezing cold weather that would make your lungs burn!" — and since track season started the day after basketball season ended, it gave her plenty of motivation to help Moravia get as far as it could in the playoffs. During her junior year, she talked her track coaches out of making her attend all the practices if she continued to compete and help the team earn points.

She was so valuable to the team, they agreed.

But during the track season in her junior year, illness managed to do something opponents on the hardwood seldom did: slow her down.

"My junior year, while competing in spring track, I got really sick with pneumonia, strep throat and mononucleosis ('kissing disease' — but I wasn't kissing people!) and ended up spending a week in the hospital flat on my back with blisters in my throat," she says. With her junior prom coming up, she was "determined to sneak out of hospital and go anyways — my dress was in the closet in my room — but I was too sick to pull it off."

Missing prom was one thing, but missing her annual trek to summer basketball camps was a whole different story.

"The doctor told me that I needed to cancel all my basketball camps for the summer, or risk heart damage," she says. "I tried to compromise and delayed going until July, but I remember having zero energy and being really frustrated that I could barely get out of bed for school. But I still managed to hit several weeks in July and August."

Senior year

Molly was fine by the time her senior season rolled around, as the team got another new coach — its third in four years. Molly has fond memories of playing for Ivan Hankins, calling him "a real great guy" with a simple philosophy: "Don't let anything rattle you on the court. Be tough, but be a lady."

"He made my last year so much fun."

Molly made it fun for Moravia fans, as well, turning up her game yet another notch. She put together a five-game stretch in which she scored 60, 76, 69, 50 and 83 points, twice eclipsing her own school record as Moravia won 14 of its first 16 games. But according to Hankins, her 83-point masterpiece wasn't even her best game of the season.

"She's had two games in which she's hit shots at the buzzer to win it for us," he told the Des Moines Tribune. "Against Mormon Trail of Garden Grove, we had four starters out with the flu. Molly picked up the slack in that one, scoring 69 points and winning the game at the buzzer."

Hankins called Molly "an absolute pleasure to coach" — a player with "a great appreciation for the fact that there are five other girls who make it happen on the court."

Meanwhile, she had to endure heckling from fans of opposing teams who didn't want her to succeed. As the *Union* observed: "Having an athletic star with a popular statewide following is a difficult position for the school or the individual. ... If such a star fouls or stubs her toe, it appears to be a delight to opponents. If a free throw is missed, it is sheer delight to the star's foes. There are often jeers for any such star if an outstanding play is pulled off."

At first, the razzing got to her. Molly remembers being booed and going back to the team huddle on the sidelines almost in tears during a timeout. "I was like, 'They don't like me! What did I do to deserve getting booed by the crowd?'"

The criticism even found its way into the press, with an opinion piece accusing her of being "overly dramatic on the court" and having a "narcissistic complex."

"Of course, that set off other people writing stuff, both for and against me."

But her coach reassured her: It was a *good* thing they didn't like her, he said, because it meant she was the reason their team was losing.

"I learned from Hankins not to show any emotional reaction to that on the court, as everyone was watching me," Molly says. "I had very humble beginnings, and humility was something I genuinely felt regardless of all the attention. But that feeling of not being good enough was always there, and even with some of my best games I would replay in my head and think about what I could have done better. I wanted people to like me, and especially my teammates."

But there were perks to being the star player, too: "Maybe for me the best part is starting with that first game turning 16, I had a date almost every Saturday night and never had to walk home from school again."

The Mohawkettes really hit their stride with a 109-62 rout of Leon on Dec. 13, with Molly scoring 54 points and getting a boost from teammate Kandi Kaster, who had 36. The game served as a tune-up for their biggest game of the year to date: a meeting with archrival Wayne just four days before Christmas. Wayne — the same team that had halted their run to the previous year's state tournament — came into the game as the state's 15th-ranked team and had already beaten the Mohawkettes earlier in the season, 71-52. Molly had been "held" to 36 points in that game, so she had plenty of motivation to help avenge her team's only loss of the season to date.

"The team was focused all week on this game, and a big school pep rally was held on game day with skits and poems of how were going to 'Beat Wayne!' So the excitement and hype over this game was at an all-time high," Molly recalls. "It was the last game before Christmas break, on a Friday night in front of a packed home crowd."

Such games often fail to live up to expectations, but this one more than did.

"It was a tight, competitive match all the way through, and our crowd was deafening in the small gym," Molly says, calling it "the most memorable game my senior year and probably in high school."

Neither side could manage more than a four-point lead in the first half, but each team threatened to pull away after intermission: The Falconettes built a seven-point advantage in the third quarter, only to see Moravia roar back and take a seven-point lead of its own in the fourth. But Wayne wasn't done: The visitors pulled within one, and then Rhonda Cobb sank a long jumper to give them the lead with 37 seconds left.

The Mohawkettes played for the last shot, with forwards Kandi and Sheri Kaster passing the ball between them and, finally, to Molly.

The clock showed 6 seconds left, and running.

"As the clock ticked down to 3 seconds, I made a move and put in a jump shot to win by one point," Molly says. "It was a moment I will never forget. I found myself at the bottom of a team dogpile while the crowd went wild. It was such a big win for us, and I got two weeks over Christmas break to enjoy the moment. Then it was back to work!"

Molly wound up with 40 points on 15 of 31 from the field and 10 of 11 free throws.

After the holiday break, she came back even hotter: She celebrated the new year by scoring 60 points in a 78-56 drubbing of Southeast Warren on Jan. 7 and followed that up three days later with a school-record 76 points. The Mohawkettes topped Seymour in that one with their first 100-point game of the new year, 101-73. With fellow forward Kandi Kaster out of the lineup with an injured knee, Molly racked up all but 10 of her team's points in a 79-77 victory over Mormon Trail on Jan. 14.

Then, a week later, with Kandi back in the lineup, Molly scored 83 for another school record in a 97-55 romp over of Leon.

Molly's heroics drew the attention of a Des Moines TV station, which sent a three-person camera crew out to shoot footage of the Mohawkettes in a home-court rematch with Mormon Trail. Moravia bolted out to a 10-0 lead, but Mormon Trail erased that early advantage with a 22-10 run, and the game remained close from that point forward. The visitors scored a basket with 1:05 remaining to take a 95-94 lead, and Moravia milked the clock for the last shot.

Molly, who had scored 70 points for the fourth time in her career, was supposed to take it, but instead the ball went to the team's No. 3 forward, who had scored just four points in the game.

She shot.

And missed.

Molly and her teammates ran to the locker room, where she broke down sobbing on the floor. The cameras captured it all, and the footage later showed up in a profile of Molly on *NBC SportsWorld*.

"I *always* kept my composure on the court, but I had no idea the cameras would come into our girls locker room and was mortified seeing that later," she says. "Obviously, losing was a bit hard for me to handle!"

Moravia went on to win the sectional tournament, as Molly scored 40 points in a 70-56 win over Twin Cedars, and hopes were high for a spot in the state tournament's "Sweet Sixteen."

Defensive teammate Lisa Clark Fetters with Molly after their last game together as Mohawkettes, a 1975 all-star game.

That would mean a trip to Des Moines, where they tourney was played, and a week off from school to visit the big city.

"They would caravan you out of town and up to Des Moines," Molly says. "They put your pictures in the store windows, and you'd be out of school for a week, and go shopping and eat in the restaurants there."

To get there, Moravia would have to get past just one more opponent: Chariton.

The Chargers had the home-court advantage, but Moravia built an early nine-point lead and was on top 20-13 at the end of the first quarter. Chariton, however, rallied to outscore the Mohawkettes 22-14 in the second period and take a one-point lead at halftime. The Chargers held a three-point lead in the fourth quarter when they went into a stall before adding a last-second bucket to win 79-74.

Molly scored 51 points in the game, making more than half her shots from the field and five of her six free throws in what turned out to be her final high school game. Moravia finishing the season at 20-5 for the second straight year, with Molly the only player on the court for all 25 games. She finished the season averaging 54.8 points and 5.4 rebounds, shooting just a hair under 50 percent from the field and 73.6 percent from the foul line.

Her 1,370 points that year ranked her 17th in Iowa history at the time for 6-on-6 girls basketball.

Her dream did come true to play at Vets Auditorium where the state basketball tournament was held every year, but it wasn't for the high school championship: It was the home court of the Iowa Cornets. In 1986, Molly did make it to the televised state championship game, and was inducted at halftime into the Iowa Basketball Hall of Fame.

Team photo from Molly's freshman year at Grand View, from left. Front: Terry Sellers, Laura Risvold, Terri Moore, Kathy Carson, Mary Jo Thola, Kim Meyer, Stephanie Bingham, Penny Brown, Back: Coach Rod Lein, Lori Gabriel, Deb Coates, Julie Biddle, Mary Aswegan, Rhonda Penquite, Joyce Elder, Lynda Johnson, Molly.

A Grand View

After her senior year at Moravia High, Molly received an invitation to take part in tryouts for the U.S. National Team that would be playing at the Pan American Games. The games, to be held that fall in Mexico City, were a tune-up for the following year's Olympics, where women's basketball would be a medal sport for the first time. The team chosen for the Pan Am Games would be the core of the '76 Olympic team.

Molly and Joyce Elder — an all-state forward from the Des Moines area — were the only high school players from Iowa at the tryouts, which were held at Lawrence, Kansas. (Coates didn't attend; she was busy playing softball during the summer.)

A total of 37 players tried out for the 12-woman team, and Elder — who would go on to play alongside Molly at Grand View College — said she didn't expect to make it.

"I would be very, very shocked if I even make it past the first cut," Elder said before the camp began. "Molly and I are the two youngest girls here, and I definitely know we're the only ones who haven't played 5-on-5."

Molly was shocked just to have been invited right out of high school, having never even played full-court basketball in her life.

"I was so intimidated," she says. "When they selected me as one of these few players to go to the trials, I was numb with shock."

She immediately set out to prepare for the challenge.

"Hankins held the gym open and helped me for several weeks to practice and prepare the best I could," she says. "However, I didn't have any chance to actually play full-court 5-on-5, since I mostly had to practice on my own and was focusing on my ball handling."

The tryouts took place in two stages: The first, Molly recalls, was a short session (she remembers it as being perhaps just a single day) at Lawrence. Then, if you made the cut there, you would be invited to a longer, full-fledged tryout camp at the University of Central Missouri. The team would be chosen in three stages, with the initial group of 37 being reduced to 20, and a final group of 15 ultimately being chosen.

When it came time to make the first cut and decide which players would be going on to Central Missouri, Molly listened as other players' names were called, one by one. There were just a few slots left when she heard her own name announced.

Several other players she knew and admired, some of whom had mentored her at summer camps, didn't make it.

"I was stunned to hear my name, one of the last called. I remember standing in the small group selected to go the final trials, looking back at the group and wondering how the heck was I picked over my camp counselors, whom I looked up to so much as a young player."

Molly went home, then returned to the court for the final tryouts a seek or two later. This was a longer trial, with players staying overnight for several days in dorm rooms at the university.

Although Molly didn't realize it at the time, several future Hall of Famers were among those competing for a spot on the team: future Tennessee coach Pat Summitt, UCLA star Ann Meyers, New York high school star Nancy Lieberman, Gail Marquis, Charlotte Lewis, Patricia Roberts and Lusia Harris.

Lewis would later play with Molly on the Iowa Cornets in the Women's Basketball League, while Lieberman, Harris, Roberts and Meyers would also play in the WBL (Roberts with Minnesota and St. Louis, Lieberman with Dallas, Meyers with New Jersey, and Harris with Houston).

"One of the players I became friends with, and who helped me navigate this new experience, was Janie Fincher who played for Chicago in the WBL," Molly says. "It took Janie and I awhile to realize that is when we first met, because the next time I saw her after those tryouts was in the WBL."

Most of the players were older than Molly, who was still just 17; Cherri Rapp, the captain of several national teams, was 25, and Molly was one of only four girls at the camp with no college experience. Most of the players were also taller than she was: "It was really the land of the giants down there," she said at the time. "Most of the girls were over 6 feet tall, and a lot of them were about 6-foot-5."

Unlike the summer camps, Molly didn't have to raise money to make the trip: Everything was paid for.

The camp was rugged, with a lot more physical contact than she was used to in high school

"I knew that I was the most inexperienced player on that court, but I decided to approach it as a basketball camp and learn as much as I could, since I would be playing this full-court game in college," Molly says. "Before I was eventually sent home, the coaches actually sat me down and told me that they had been so impressed with my scoring records that they purposely brought me to the finals so I would get the experience. I remember being so grateful to have had that chance, I was not that disappointed to be going home."

She had some trouble *getting* home, however. Bus difficulties left her stuck in Kansas City for four hours late at night with only $1 left in her pocket, but she managed to make it back in one piece.

A couple of weeks later, she reported to Grand View College in Des Moines to help with the summer basketball camp there. Molly had accepted a scholarship to attend Grand View after also considering Centerville. As it turns out, future Iowa Cornets assistant coach Bruce Mason recommended her.

"A friend of mine asked me if I would go to Moravia to officiate a couple of basketball games with him," Mason recalls. "The girls game was a shootout. with the final score being something like 96-94. I was coaching an adult women's AAU team at the time with Rod Lein, who was coaching at Grand View at the time.

"I admired Molly's pure shooting technique. Her team never got to the Iowa State Tournament, so she never got a lot of exposure. When I got back to Ankeny, I told Rod that there was a player in Moravia that he needed to contact. Rod contacted Molly and she ended up playing at Grand View."

At one point, Molly thought she might end up playing for Bob Spencer, her former camp director, at William Penn, which at the time had the top program in Iowa, but it didn't work out that way.

"I think Bob Spencer had always planned to recruit me to play college ball for him," she says, "but he was loaded with talent and didn't want me to sit on the bench, so he told me that he wanted me to go to Grand View for two years then transfer to his program for my last two years. While at Grand View, we somehow played William Penn in some tournament and *beat* them — so, needless to say, I hoped he was sorry he passed on having me in his program."

On to college

Instead, she ended up playing for Rod Lein, who would later serve as general manager (and interim coach) for the Cornets.

"Rod was very bold in his recruiting and game scheduling. He came to one of my high school games and told me, 'You're going to be my next point guard. How would you like to play with Deb Coates and travel the country?' I actually hadn't given much thought to college — I was enjoying high school ball so much I could barely stand the thought of it being over.

"I wasn't that thrilled about playing 'boys rules' 5-on-5. But I wasn't anywhere near done playing when my team was beat out of going to state. Rod's offer sounded like fun, and Des Moines is only about 90 minutes from Moravia."

Grand View was coming off a 25-4 season but had just one starter returning from a team that had been decimated by injuries and eligibility problems the year before. By the time the Vikings reached their next-to-last game that season, they had just five players left from an initial roster of 12, and Lein put just four of them on the court at one point during a game against Kansas when one needed to come out for a breather.

The Vikings walloped the Jayhawks anyway, 73-34, but lost their final game when their third player fouled with 3 seconds left against William Penn, leaving just two players on the court. Despite the disadvantage, the score was just 65-52 at the time.

Still, it was clear the Vikings needed to reload.

Lein started virtually from scratch with 14 incoming freshmen. Three of them, however, had averaged better than 45 points a game as seniors in Iowa: Coates (55.4), Molly (54.8) and Elder (45.5). Lein said he'd have to platoon them, calling the group "the best talent ever at Grand View."

"We had a combined scoring average of 200 points a game (from high school) on the same team," Molly says. "We all ended up averaging in double figures." She added that it was "a dream come true" to play with Coates at Grand View, "but also Joyce Elder, who was a highly respected player who had been to the state tournament."

Rhonda Penquite, the lone returning starter, had averaged 21 points the previous year and had been chosen to an All-America squad, was optimistic about the team's chances for success: "With the kind of athletes we have here now, we definitely should be a top-notch team," she told the Des Moines Tribune. "I've never seen so many good shooters on the same team."

Many universities weren't offering scholarships for women's basketball at the time, but Grand View was able to do so because it was privately funded. The school was still a junior college, but was in the midst of transitioning into a four-year institution when Molly arrived.

Still, its program had a head start on many major universities, and it showed.

As the season got under way, Coates scored 16 points and Molly dropped in 13 as Grand View topped the University of Nebraska in its opener, 76-66.

Molly led the way with 21 points in a 95-80 triumph over Missouri the following week, and she had 21 more to lead all scorers once again in a 93-64 rout of Northwest Missouri the week after that. That win put the Vikings into the championship game of an eight-team "Turkey Tournament" hosted by Southwest Missouri State. Their opponent: Kansas State, the nation's sixth-ranked team.

Grand View nearly pulled off an upset against the Wildcats, building a 37-32 lead at halftime before falling by a single point, 73-72. The Vikings led 72-72 before K-State tied it with 2 seconds left. The game appeared headed toward overtime, but Grand View was assessed a technical foul for calling a timeout when it had none remaining; Kansas State hit the resulting free throw to seal the win. Molly again led the way for the Vikings, this time with 16 points.

"I remember being a bit in awe stepping onto that court with a large crowd and playing as hard as we could in every game," Molly says of her college experience.

But it didn't show in the results.

In all, Grand View won 13 of its first 15 games, including a 112-53 romp over the University of Iowa and a 69-36 pounding of Minnesota. The Vikings ran into a buzz saw when they faced defending national champion Delta State, falling 80-50, but rebounded with a 71-68 win over previously unbeaten (14-0) Mississippi.

Molly sends the ball toward the basket during a Grand View game.

Both games were part of a swing through the South that Lein had scheduled to pit Grand View against the best teams in the country. In fact, the Vikings played 11 of the top 20 teams in the nation that year. This was during an era before the NCAA governed women's sports: During the 1970s, they were the province of an organization called the Association for Intercollegiate Athletics for Women, or AIAW.

"Rod knew he had recruited the best of the best Iowa high school players and wanted to prove we could play with anyone with our tough schedule — keep in mind this was before NCAA stepped into women's college basketball," Molly says. "So, he scheduled a long road trip to the Deep South, including a game against Delta State, who won the AIAW National Championship three years in a row from 1975-77."

The trip had its moments.

"The traveling was a bit rough with all of us packed into a

van pulling a trailer with all our suitcases," Molly recalls. "To save money, Rod had arranged for us to stay with the host team a time or two. One of the games got really screwed up at the scorer's table in regards to keeping the points and fouls accurate. Rod protested several times, and it was fixed, but it happened again."

During the game, played at Memphis, Penquite recalls that the Vikings had 59 points and scored a basket, but instead of clicking forward to 61, it went backward to 51. "Their player fouled out, and she came back in," she adds. "They said she had only four fouls."

Molly continues: "It was a series of mistakes that kept stopping the game, and the refs weren't very supportive," she says. "So, with about 5 minutes left in the game, he pulled us off the floor. We left and had no hotel, as we were supposed to stay with the other team. I remember driving for a couple hours after the game and Rod rented *one* hotel room that we all piled into. So, it was definitely an adventure."

That wasn't the only mishap.

"As were driving to another game, I looked back and noticed our trailer was gone and said, 'Hey Rod, our trailer isn't following us anymore!' And, sure enough, we turned around and drove back a ways, and there was the trailer in a field with our stuff all over the place. What I remember is everyone laughing at me while I insisted on finding every one of my electric hair curlers spread around that field."

Grand View made it to the semifinals of the state's AIAW tournament before falling to Northern Iowa 85-79.

The team then qualified for the small college national tournament in Ashland, Ohio, by beating Tarkio College of Missouri 82-75 at a regional event in Nebraska. But by that time, the Vikings were without a head coach: Lein had accepted an offer to form a new program at Simpson College, and Grand View had relieved him of his duties immediately after discovering he was trying to get some of his Viking players to jump ship along with him.

Molly didn't consider it for a second. She liked her classes at Grand View and the campus, and the team was still solid.

"When word got out that he was talking to Grand View players about transferring to Simpson, he was promptly fired," Molly says. "So, there we were, bound for a National Tournament with *no* coach. The gymnastics coach, Charles Jacobson, and the men's basketball coach, Dave Sisam drove the team to the tournament, ran practices and helped us as much as they could. While it was a fun experience, it just wasn't the same and we didn't play nearly as well as we could have."

The team brought a 26-6 record into the tournament but lost to Francis Marion of South Carolina 69-68 in the opening round. Molly led Grand View with 14 points, but the Vikings were called for 20 fouls to just eight for the Patriots.

"We were staying in college dorm rooms, and I remember it being pretty hot and humid, then one night all the power went out in town, interrupting the tournament," Molly remembers. "It was so surreal, almost like a horror movie, when everything went dark and we were all running around."

Taking a break

It would be the last time Molly would play competitive basketball for more than a year, as her personal life intervened: She married Dennie Bolin in the summer and had a son, Damien, the following year.

"At the end of the season, it seemed like all of the team had scattered," she says.

Elder moved over to Central Missouri, Penquite moved on to Oral Roberts University, and Coates enrolled at Iowa Wesleyan College in Mount Pleasant. Meanwhile, 6-foot-4 center Mary Aswegan had been ruled academically ineligible. The new coach, Jerry Slater, didn't have time to do much recruiting and was left with a bare-bones squad going forward.

There just weren't the opportunities for women to continue in the sport back then, and there were plenty of people out there trying to discourage them: Think more practically, they said; settle down or look for something stable to make a living.

Among them was Bud McLearn, who coached prep powerhouse Mediapolis to a 333-8 record on its home court, including winning streaks of 97 and 84 games. Coates was one of his players.

"I was shocked to see quotes from Bud McLearn, who was the camp director for the Camp of the Champs I attended, about the futility of girls high school players continuing in college. His star player and my peer, Deb Coates, came to Grand View as probably the most famous high school player on the team after playing in two televised state high school championships. When she left Grand View after one season, I don't think she played college basketball again and didn't try out for the Iowa Cornets.."

Molly almost hung up her sneakers for good, too.

"That summer, I got married and didn't come back to the team either," Molly says. "Grand View went 1-20 that year. Thankfully, all my financial aid was in place, and I was able to attend Year 2 at Grand View without a basketball scholarship. Since I was living off campus, I also received a nice check each semester for expenses, and that was so helpful — and ensured that I would not have to quit college."

Dennie Bolin, a bricklayer and bass player in a local band

who had graduated two years ahead of her, had been Molly's boyfriend in Moravia, and she'd broken up with him before going away to college. But he'd continued to visit her at Grand View and she'd wound up going back to Moravia every weekend. Eventually, he won her over: "He was just too persistent, and we ended up getting married."

Molly took a month off of school during the spring semester of 1977 to have her son and didn't play basketball at Grand View — or anywhere. Instead, she focused on her studies as she pursued a degree in communications.

"When school started up again, I was able to find a good babysitter and arrange my schedule so I was only gone about a half a day, three days a week," she says. "However, I was taking TV production classes and began doing color commentary for the home basketball games for a local cable channel. I loved it and thought that was the career I wanted to go into."

Perhaps her most memorable experience during this period ended with her mistakenly winding up in the men's locker room after a game.

"One night, the men's game had finished and we had gone to commercial and only had to finish with the game summary wrap-up. I accidentally spilled a Coke on our announcer table. In a panic, I jumped up and ran to the women's locker room to get some paper towels to do a quick cleanup before going back on camera.

"I went flying into the locker room and was at the paper towel dispenser before I realized the visiting men's team was using the women's locker room, and they were in the process of showering — without clothes! I ran out of there faster than I had run in, cleaned the mess on the table, and finished the broadcast with a bright red face. Then I managed to hide before any of those players came out of the locker room."

But Molly couldn't hide from her love of basketball. She almost quit altogether, but then one afternoon, she was invited to play in a church league pickup game.

"I went to a pickup game with a church league and scored 60 points," she recalls. "I thought, 'That was too easy. I've got to go back and play again.'"

So, she did.

She was back on the court when the Vikings kicked off their 1977-78 season with an 83-60 win over Westmar, scoring 15 points as the No. 2 scorer in that victory. But the team wasn't the powerhouse it had been two years earlier, when Grand View had beaten Iowa by nearly 50 points. This time out, the Vikings fell to the Hawkeyes 88-73 in their fourth game of the season, despite team-high 26 points from Molly. It was a similar story against Nebraska, which edged Grand View 84-81 despite Molly's 29 points — nine of them coming in 3 minutes during a late rally that fell just short.

"It was an all-new team with a lot of freshman Iowa players learning 5-on-5," Molly recalls.

With many of her teammates from the 1975-76 team having left to play at other schools, she wound up taking the floor against some of them.

Something else had changed, as well: Molly had a young son now, and sometimes, she would bring him to games and practices.

"He doesn't bother anybody," coach Jerry Slater said. "I'm just glad Molly came back to play with us."

For good reason: By late January, Molly was averaging 22.3 points a game, even though the Vikings were still struggling with a 7-12 record. Still, she wasn't about to give up on the season: She turned things up another notch against Iowa State on Feb. 1, tossing in 42 points and sealing an 85-82 upset by sinking a pair of free throws in the final minute. It was the biggest point total of her college career.

Clearly, she had not only acclimated to the 5-on-5 game, but mastered it.

"For an Iowa girl, she's the best penetrator I've seen," Slater told the *Des Moines Tribune*. "Most Iowa girls can't penetrate, but she really can."

Just as she had at Moravia High, Molly was carrying the team, becoming the first player in Grand View history to surpass 1,000 career points.

Grand View had hoped to get a shot at William Penn in the state tournament but fell short with an 81-69 loss to Mount Mercy, the defending champion. Molly led the Vikings with 23 points, and Grand View battled the Mustangs on even terms much of the way. The game was tied at 63 before Mount Mercy pulled away from a Grand View team slowed by the flu bug: One starter didn't suit up for the game, and another managed to play but fouled out.

The Vikings concluding the season with a 79-77 consolation win over Luther, which was duly reported on page 19 of the *Des Moines Tribune*. A story that ran a day earlier, however, would turn out to have a far bigger impact on Molly's career. It featured her former coach at Grand View, Rod Lein, who was back in the news — but this time, not as a college coach.

Lein had been talking with Bill Byrne, a sports promoter from Columbus, Ohio, who was planning to start up a professional women's basketball league. Byrne was planning a team in Iowa, to capitalize on the popularity of girls basketball there, and had secured a commitment from sporting goods entrepreneur George Nissen to invest $250,000 in the team. Nissen had already made a $10,000 payment, or 20 percent of the franchise fee.

"I was very skeptical about the league at first, but now I'm really sold on it," Lein said at the time.

After graduating from Grand View, Molly was planning to use her two years of college eligibility remaining to go south and she wanted to play for the University of Arizona to complete her education. But before she could do that, her phone rang. When she picked it up, Lein was on the other end.

"I had gone as far as I could academically (and athletically) at Grand View and graduated with a third-year certificate," Molly recalls. "At the time they only had a four-year nursing program, but were in the process of being a four-year college. I was looking into moving to Arizona to finish college and thought Dennie could work more consistently in a warmer climate. At least until I got the call from Rod, in April or May of 1978."

Lein told her he'd been hired as general manager of Iowa's new pro team, and he wanted her to try out.

She said yes.

Molly, left front, with her teammates on the 1977-78 Grand View squad

Molly became the first player signed for the Iowa Cornets and the WBL.

The First Cornet

The Women's Basketball League was the brainchild of a man who ran a pro scouting service and had served as director of player personnel for the Chicago Fire of the World Football League. More recently, in 1977, Bill Byrne had started up a national pro slow-pitch softball league for men that attracted a few former major leaguers.

Byrne was always looking for a new idea, and he became convinced that women's basketball was the next big thing. When he announced the venture, he envisioned teams in major cities like Boston, Washington, Los Angeles, New York, Detroit and Chicago. As Molly put it, however, "His ambitions exceeded his talents." Of those cities, only New York and Chicago were represented with the league tipped off in the fall of 1978.

The first team to announce it was joining the league, by contrast, represented a state without a single major pro sports team: Iowa. It was by far the smallest market in the league, but it had a couple of advantages. One was its built-in, enthusiastic fan base for girls basketball, and the other was its owner, a man named George Nissen.

"As I remember, George Nissan was a wonderful man, always providing great support of the Iowa community through his gymnastics equipment business," says Dave Almstead, who served as president of the Dallas Diamonds and, briefly, as the league's interim commissioner in its final year. "I recall him telling me that if anyone would own the Iowa team, he thought that he should be the person."

The Iowa native had been just a teenager when he'd been inspired by a trip to the circus. The trapeze artists who performed there fell into a stiff but flexible net that sent them ricocheting back upward during their routine. Nissen, a high school gymnast and diver, wondered whether he could create a similar effect to help him train, using rubber from innertubes. Teaming up with his coach, Larry Griswold, he stitched together strips of this material together and created the first trampoline, borrowing the name from the Spanish *trampolin*, for "diving board." He trademarked the name and teamed up with Griswold to start a company producing the invention, based in Cedar Rapids.

The Cornets, however, would be based in Des Moines, where they planned to play eight of their 17 home games there, at Veterans Memorial Auditorium. The team wanted to live up to its name by representing the entire state, so three games were scheduled for Cedar Rapids, with six others being played at various sites. Among them: Cedar Falls, Council Bluffs, Sioux City; high school gyms in Bettendorf and Spencer; and a junior high facility in Ottumwa, just a half-hour from Moravia. The home opener was set for Dec. 17, with the regular season concluding in early April.

Nissen's business success made him well-positioned to make the Cornets a success, as well.

"I'm not quite sure how I got into this," Nissen told *The Des Moines Register*. "It's like wrestling a bear — you can't let go."

Clearly, the owners were serious, even if the media sometimes didn't know what to make of their venture. A report by the UPI wire service in June mistakenly spelled the team's name as "Coronets," like the paper towel.

(The Cornets weren't a bunch of trumpet-playing hoopsters, either. The name was a play on Iowa's ubiquitous *corn* crop. "The word 'corn' is in there," Nissen said, "and if you put enough fertilizer on corn, it will grow." *Sports Illustrated* called Molly "the girl from the cornfields," even though she didn't come from a farming family, and maintained she "took up basketball at the age of 12 because it was what every good little Iowa girl did.")

Larry Albaugh, the team's chairman of the board, viewed the Cornets as "our only chance to be major league in anything." He wanted them to be the Green Bay Packers of women's basketball. And that's exactly what they would become: In their brief existence, the Cornets were among the league's top draws at the gate and made it to the championship series twice in as many years.

Lein set the stage for that success by formulating a plan to assemble a top-flight team. And, as the first WBL franchise to get off the ground, the Cornets had a head start on everyone else. The league was still very much a work in progress: It only had six of its 12 planned teams in place when it was announced, with Iowa joining Chicago, Milwaukee, Minnesota, New Jersey and Washington D.C. The only other team with a nickname, the Chicago Skyliners, wound up changing it to the Hustle, while Washington dropped out. The league would ultimately open the season with just eight teams instead of 12 (the others would represent Dayton, Houston and New York).

The Cornets, meanwhile, were starting to come together.

Despite Lein's experience and personal ties to Iowa, he had cast a wide net in his search for players.

"Looking back, is I don't remember any other Grand View players than Rhonda Penquite trying out for Iowa Cornets," Molly says. "Rod wanted to put together a winning team and recruited a lot of players outside of Iowa. Janie Fincher" — who ultimately signed with Chicago — "showed me a letter on Iowa Cornet letterhead inviting her to our tryout camp. I think she was living in Las Vegas at the time. Many didn't want to go to Iowa, including Janie."

Still, once they heard about the new venture, "they wanted to try out for the pro league, but looked for other teams."

Molly was one of 19 players who attended a three-day tryout camp in mid-June. The camp at Coe College in Cedar Rapids gave coach George "Nick" Nicodemus his first chance to size up the talent available to him. Nicodemus, a Des Moines native, had twice led John F. Kennedy College of Wahoo, Nebraska, to AAU women's championships before taking over as head coach at University of Nebraska for two years.

Under league rules, each team would be allowed 12 active and five inactive players on its roster.

A variety of hopefuls showed up at the camp, including Bobbi Brockhage, who traveled 3,000 miles, all the way from Alaska, where she had been coaching for the past two years. But the opportunity to get back out on the court herself was too good to pass up.

"I played probably for 10 years competitively," Brockhage, 24, told United Press International. "Now I've been away from playing for two years, but I love it. I love the game. It's a lot better than coaching. I want competition."

Brockhage didn't make the team.

Among the players who showed up to try out was Denise Long, nearly a decade after her glory days at Union-Whitten High School, where she set the national career scoring record.

"She's out of condition, and only she knows if she wants to get back into shape," Nicodemus said.

Long didn't make the team, either. (But the Cornets did sign her during their second year in an attempt to lure more fans. Long agreed, even though she was, in her own words, "an old, out-of-condition athlete sitting on the bench." During one game, the fans started demanding that the Cornets put her in. She entered the game and promptly committed a foul; her entire WBL career amounted to one point scored in 40 seconds of play.)

Nicodemus had more praise for 6-foot-3 center Susan Alt and 6-foot forward Nancy Rutter, both from the University of Missouri. Mary Schrad, a 5-9 forward from Briar Cliff College in Sioux City, was another Iowan at the camp. Also from Iowa: 6-1 forward Connie Kunzmann, who had attended Everly High School before crossing the state line to play college ball at Nebraska's Wayne State. Others attending the camp included 5-11 forward Joan Uhl from Cal Poly-Pomona, 5-10 forward Denise Sharps of Indiana State, 5-7 guard Robin Tucker of Ohio State. All seven wound up playing for the Cornets.

Tucker and Doris Draving, who also played both seasons for Iowa, would team up with Molly to become some of the most important contributors on the team: Tucker as a playmaker, and Draving — who would also join Molly in the WBL's third season on the San Francisco Pioneers — as a rebounding force.

Molly singled out the pair for praise specifically, adding: "What amazing unselfish teammates I had on the Cornets and, eventually, the (San Francisco) Pioneers! We all played for the love of the game and were in it to win it. They understood that it was far more important to me to win than set scoring records which was a byproduct of trying to win big games. It was fun to play on such a good team and bonds were formed that have turned into lifelong friendships."

Molly would also become close to Uhl and Kunzmann, who, like Draving, was a force under the basket. She came to the Cornets as the leading rebounder and second-leading scorer in Wayne State history, having averaged 20 points a game in both her junior and senior seasons.

"Connie Kunzmann was frequently my roommate on road trips, so we hung out a lot in our downtime, as well," Molly says. "She had a little handheld football video game that she played constantly, and it made the most annoying sounds! When we moved to Cedar Rapids the second year, I rented a house and had an extra bedroom that Connie moved into for several weeks until she got an apartment. She had a yellow Mustang, and we would go to practice together with the music cranked up.

"Connie was the Kurt Rambis of the Iowa Cornets, a real blue-collar worker battling under the board game after game. She also set a record of 11 steals in one game. One time we both bought Groucho Marx glasses and made a pact to wear them on the court for starting lineup introductions. We chickened out at the last minute but laughed our butts off about it."

Almost as soon the tryout camp closed, the Cornets announced they were ready to start negotiating with "six or seven players" on contracts.

Molly was one of those players.

"I've been taking 20 hours of class work, holding down a job and trying to raise a family," she said at the time. "The way I look at it, that's 10 times worse than just playing ball and having a family, which is what I'd be doing if I played pro ball."

One of the downsides would be missing the 1980 Olympics, because the rules made pro athletes ineligible to compete. A few of the top women, including Nancy Lieberman and Carol Blazejowski, didn't sign contracts with the new league because they wanted to preserve their amateur status for the Olympics. Unfortunately for them, the United States wound up boycotting the 1980 Games in Moscow to protest the Soviet invasion of Afghanistan. Team USA, which had won a silver medal it the first women's basketball competition back in 1976, wouldn't compete in the Olympics again until 1984, and that was too long for Blazejowski, Lieberman and others to wait: They signed contracts with the WBL heading into its third season.

Olympic eligibility, however, was not a concern for Molly.

"The thing I felt like I gave up is going to the University of Arizona and playing two more years down there," she says. "It didn't occur to me at the time that I would be losing out on Olympic eligibility, because the Olympics didn't have the visibility they do today."

A couple of weeks after the tryouts, Molly got a call inviting her to the Iowa governor's office for a special event: She would be the first player to sign a contract by the Cornets and, in doing so, she would be the first player ever signed to play for a women's pro basketball league. They told her: "We're going to make you the face of the team."

"Iowa Governor Robert Ray was well liked in Iowa and also was a big supporter of girls basketball," Molly says. "It was a such a huge thrill to go into his office and sit at his desk to officially sign my contract. With the room filled with cameras and reporters, I definitely realized my life had taken a big swing towards something exciting. ... Being from a small town like Moravia, that's not something that happens every day.

"Of course, it was a huge honor to be announced as the first player to sign with the first team in the first women's pro basketball league, but it was much later in life before I truly appreciated the significance of that."

A week later, the Cornets signed Crevier, Sharps and Tucker, giving them four players on their roster; of the four, only Molly was from Iowa. At 5-foot-3, Crevier was the league's shortest player. By the time she joined the team, she was already known for her ballhandling skills and was performing for audiences in the area.

In fact, that's how she drew Nissen's attention. "I was invited to perform my basketball handling show at the girls state high school basketball tournament in Iowa," she says. "The new owner of the Iowa Cornets saw me perform and invited me to try out for the Iowa Cornets. I went to a tryout and made the team."

Others soon followed. Much later, Molly realized that some of them were being paid far more than she was. She speculates that perhaps they were offered larger contracts as an incentive to play in Iowa instead of a larger market, such as New York or Chicago (where Janie Fincher wound up).

"In the early days of the Iowa Cornets, I was pretty naïve to things unless it was right in front of my face," she says. "They actually signed me for about $900 a month, which I didn't learn until years later was half of what they were offering some of the other girls."

In addition to Molly and the seven other players who aced

the tryout, the roster included Crevier, a 5-foot-3 guard and ballhandling wizard from South Dakota State, and Draving, a 6-1 center from East Stoudsburg State in Pennsylvania, both of whom would also join her on the San Francisco Pioneers. Draving even had some experience playing 6-on-6 basketball: Her high school in Philadelphia played a variation that featured two guards, two rovers and two forwards in 1969 before switching to the 5-on-5 game in 1970.

Rounding out the roster were D.K. Thomas, a 5-11 forward from Stephen F. Austin in Texas; 5-4 guard Anita "Sister" Green from the College of Charleston; and Kathy Hawkins, a 5-6 guard from the University of Nebraska. At 20 years of age, Molly was the youngest of the bunch.

She made an immediate impression. Tucker recalls her first encounter with Molly: "We were at the first tryout for the Iowa Cornets at Coe College in Cedar Rapids, Iowa. Myself and Joan Uhl, an All-American player from Cal Poly-Pomona, were on the far end of the court shooting to warm up. Molly came walking in, I believe with Rod Lein, the general manager. Molly was dressed to play, but her hair wasn't pulled back and she looked a little like Farrah Fawcett. Joan looked at me and said, 'What is she here for? A lipstick commercial?'"

The Cornets organized a couple of scrimmages in Mississippi and prepared for the start of the season.

But the team they would face in the league's first championship series, the Houston Angels, got a later start. They were coached by Don Knodel, who had spent eight seasons coaching the men's team at Rice University, where his assistant, Greg Williams had been one of his players from 1967 to '69. Williams, who was named co-MVP of the Southwest Conference in his senior season, joined Knodel's staff as a student assistant the following year.

"We were throwing this thing together, literally day by day," Williams recalls.

Owner Hugh Sweeney wasn't a basketball guy, so when he picked the No. 1 draft position out of a hat, he picked UCLA star Ann Meyers "because he had seen her picture on the cover of *Sports Illustrated*," he says.

It was a solid choice, but Meyers declined to play for the Angels that season, still hoping to play in the 1980 Olympics.

The Angels didn't even get to play any exhibition games. The closest they came was an informal scrimmage against some people from Knodel's workplace: Both he and Williams had day jobs in sales, so the team could only practice at night. But Williams did manage a trip to Mississippi for a look at the Cornets in one of *their* exhibition games, which is where he caught his first glimpse of Molly.

"She was fun to watch and she brought an excitement to the game that is just is very rare," he says.

The Cornets, however, weren't coming together as a team under Nicodemus.

"We'll be a winner," he had declared upon taking the job in March. "I haven't practiced being a loser."

The Cornets were winners, all right, but the 53-year-old Nicodemus wasn't part of it: Just four days before the team's season opener at Minnesota, he was sacked. Lein chalked it up to a "personal conflicts and personal differences with the players," and took Nicodemus' place on the sidelines as interim coach. He remained in charge, with Bruce Mason staying on as assistant, for about three months before Dan Moulton — a former Iowa high school coach — was hired as a permanent replacement.

Nicodemus, Molly says, "was hired because of his long history of coaching in Iowa, but as I remember, he spent too long of a portion of practice lecturing us while we sat. As the season approached, we were not even close to being ready to play — I'm not sure if some girls complained or Rod saw what was going on — but he realized George was not going to work out."

Just a few days after the Cornets cut him loose, Nicodemus got a job as head coach of the rival Milwaukee Does, who had fired Candace Klinzing after just a single game. Klinzing herself had replaced the team's original coach, Charlotte Adams, who had left before the season even started because of an illness in the family.

But Nicodemus didn't last long in Milwaukee, either, as the Does fired him five weeks into his tenure there after an abysmal 1-9 start. (It might not have been entirely Nicodemus' fault: During the Does' two seasons in the league, they finished last in the Midwest Division both times.)

From benchwarmer to star

The rest of the league eventually came together. Most of the rules would mirror those used in the NBA: There would be a 24-second shot clock, four 12-minute quarters, and a limit of six personal fouls per player each game. There was no 3-point shot during the first season, but it would be added in the second. And there were a couple of important differences between the men's and women's games. First, the lane would be just 12 feet wide, as in college basketball, rather than 16, as in the NBA. Second, the ball would be smaller.

Karen Logan, who had played three years with a barnstorming team called the All-American Red Heads, signed with the Chicago Hustle and also designed the league's innovative ball. Used for the first time in the WBL, it was 1.5

inches less in circumference and 3 ounces lighter than a regulation NBA ball. It would eventually became standard for the women's game.

"I *loved* it," Molly says. "I had so much more hand control, and the few ounces lighter convinced me I could shoot further out."

Other changes involved how many teams would be involved and where they would play. The Dayton Rockettes replaced Washington in the league after the D.C. franchise was unable to find a place to play.

A draft was held July 17 in New York City and produced some colorful selections: New York chose Phyllis George, a former Miss America then serving as a commentator for CBS Sports. And Chicago picked Sandy Allen, the tallest woman in the world at 7-foot-7.

Other picks were more realistic: Chicago took Rita Easterling, an All-American from Mississippi College, with the No. 1 overall free-agent pick. Houston chose two of the biggest names in Delta State center Lusia Harris and UCLA standout Ann Meyers, who was the top draft pick among college seniors. New Jersey selected Carol Blazejowski, a highly touted 5-10 forward from Montclair State; New York took 6-2 center Althea Gywn from Queens College.

Easterling would live up to her billing, earning MVP honors for both the first season and the inaugural All-Star Game, and Gwyn would be a three-time all-star, pacing the WBL with 17.3 rebounds a game and ranking third in scoring at 23 points during the league's first season.

But the other names on that list all passed on the first season. Meyers and Harris would play in the second season, while Blazejowski would come aboard for the third.

Despite her status as the league's first player to sign, Molly wasn't on the list.

She wasn't on the court much early on, either.

In the season's first game, Chicago won 92-87 at Milwaukee before a crowd of 7,800, as Easterling set a single-game record for assists at 21 that would stand the test of time. The Cornets won their opener 103-81 at Minnesota before 4,100 fans, but Molly hit just one basket and made 1 of 2 free throws for three points. Joan Uhl led the way with 22, while Molly's former teammate at Grand View, Rhonda Penquite, had 14 to go with 13 rebounds.

It was the start of a frustrating month for Molly, who wound up watching most of the action from the bench as Iowa won its first four games to take the lead in the Midwest Division, while Houston won four of its first five to set the pace in the East.

Despite her high-profile signing, Molly started the Cornets' first season deep on the bench, about the 12th player in the rotation. In one game she failed to score, playing just 4 minutes and not even taking a shot. Through December, she'd played just 42 minutes, the second-fewest on the team.

"It was a rough start to my pro basketball career," she recalls.

When Nicodemus was fired and Lein took over before the first game, she might have expected to get more playing time. After all, Lein had coached her at Grand View, where she had consistently been his leading scorer in games against four-year universities.

But it didn't turn out that way.

"With a last-minute coaching change just prior to the first game, I had no idea what to expect or what role on the team was expected of me," she says. "As Rod took over the coaching, I did expect to play, because he knew what I could do since he recruited me to Grand View. But we had a team full of good athletes from all over the country, and the coaches must have felt that four years of college experience made them more ready for the pro game than me after my two non-consecutive seasons at Grand View."

Another issue was Lein's new strategy of platooning players, five at a time, with each unit playing half of each 12-minute quarter. The idea, Molly says, was to have fresh players on the court at all times so the Cornets could wear out opponents with a fast-paced game. The problem was, as the 12th player in the rotation, Molly didn't make it into either the first *or* the second unit.

"Rod eventually told me he wanted me to be the team's 'designated shooter,'" she says, "and would put me in cold for a few minutes here and there for 'quick scores.' Anyone who has played basketball knows that points generally come in the flow of the game, and it helps to be warmed up to pop in 15-foot jumpers. Plus, I had not been a substitute since I was a ninth-grader, and though outwardly I was supportive of my teammates, on the inside I was miserable."

Her lowly status created a vicious circle: She couldn't get enough playing time to get into a shooting rhythm, so she missed more shots than usual, which only reaffirmed the coaches' perception that she wasn't ready for more minutes on the court. Through December, she was shooting just 19 percent from the field.

"For the first two months of the season, I was stuck in a rut and on the bench, and didn't know how to change it," she explains. "The short bursts of playing time off the bench also wreaked havoc on my shooting percentage, so the coaches seemed to get less and less confident of putting me on the court. I did play in every game, but my stats from my limited time on the court only reinforced my low position on the team."

Shortly before Christmas, Lein put her in against Chicago with the Cornets trailing. She hit her first three shots, and Iowa went on to win the game.

"That gave her a lot of confidence," Lein said at the time. "It was a gamble, but Molly made up her mind that she was going to play. She found out she didn't like sitting on the bench. She just wants to play. That's the difference."

Actually, Molly had *never* liked sitting on the bench. She'd just needed the opportunity to help the team win. Soon enough, she was able to do more than that. But even team owner George Nissen was skeptical.

"When I told Mr. Nissen I was going to start her recently, he said, 'No, not her,'" Lein said at the time.

Molly quickly proved Nissen wrong in the most emphatic way possible. On Jan. 28 in Des Moines, she got off to a slow start, scoring just 2 points in the first half because, as usual, she wasn't playing much. But then, starter Denise Sharps went down with a knee injury before halftime, and Lein made a decision: He would insert Molly into the lineup to start the second half.

"Rod came up to me at halftime and said, 'Be ready: You are starting the second half.' I couldn't believe it. I was so excited, as I had been waiting a long time for this chance to play."

She made the most of it, pouring in a league-record 38 points in the second half on 13 of 19 from the floor and a perfect 14-for-14 at the foul line. The result: a 116-105 victory over the Milwaukee Does. Her 40 total points set a league record.

"That opened the floodgates for my playing time, and from that point forward I was an important part of the team," she says.

Even Molly, who had been used to scoring in bunches during her high school and college days, seemed surprised: "I can't believe I scored 40 points," she said afterward, downplaying the achievement by adding, "There were a lot of free throws and layups."

But there was no downplaying her continued scoring achievements as the season progressed. Sharps' injury wasn't serious: She was back in the lineup when the Cornets visited Minnesota on Feb. 3 and scored 23 points in a 109-106 loss to the Fillies. But Molly added 20 points of her own and nearly saved the day for Iowa by hitting a 15-foot jumper with 1 second left to force an overtime.

She was starting to click with point guard Robin Tucker, who led the Cornets with 207 assists that first season.

"Molly and I communicated well on the court," Tucker recalls. "She was quick with a V-cut or back-door cut, and during the game, we could evaluate the defense and know which cuts or screens would get her open. It was my job to get it in her hands immediately as she broke loose so she could get the shot off or, if they were running toward her to catch up, drive by."

On March 27, Molly surpassed her 40-point effort with 53 in a 126-109 homecourt win over Minnesota. She didn't even start the game, entering midway through the first quarter, but she didn't take long to get warmed up, finishing with 19 baskets on 25 attempts from the floor. It was not only a personal best, but another league record — one she would break twice more the following season, when she scored 50 or more three times.

In fact, Molly's four 50-point games account for half of those ever produced in the first four decades of major women's pro basketball and two-thirds recorded in the WBL (Carol Blazejowski and Liz Silcott each had one, and Molly's top two games are *still* better than the WNBA record as of this writing, four decades later.)

"Molly came into the pro league, married and a young mother having played only two years at Grand View," Tucker says. "She was an unknown on the national scene and yet managed to score 50-plus points repeatedly against the best players in the nation."

One aspect of her game coaches sometimes criticized was her defense, but even in Iowa's 6-on-6 high school game, she had averaged about five steals a game — a figure that's even more impressive since she was playing almost exclusively on offense. Her defense developed further when she switched to the 5-on-5 format in college, and it only improved during her pro years. A video from 1984, for instance, shows her covering rival superstar Nancy Lieberman like a blanket all over the court.

"My biggest issue was I never had a good (defensive) coach (until) Kirk actually taught position on the floor" and help defense, Molly says. "Man-to-man defense doesn't work for anyone without help team defense. I was certainly quick and aggressive enough, but it was more about learning positioning."

Doris Draving recalls the criticism as well: "The coaches used to get on Molly's case about her defense in the beginning, but she improved greatly over time," she says.

According to Draving, Molly had an "ability to steal the inbounds pass and score a quick layup when we needed a bucket." Then, of course, there was her "tremendous accuracy" shooting: "When Molly was hot from the outside, she was on fire and couldn't miss."

By the time Molly produced her 53-point game, she had a new nickname: "Machine Gun Molly," bestowed on her by Thomas Boswell in a *Washington Post* feature story on the WBL that ran March 3.

"Modern day, she'd be AK-47," then-Houston Angels

assistant Greg Williams quips.

It took some time for Molly to get used to the name.

"I didn't really get a choice, as the press, and then the teams started using it," she says. "To me, just not as cool as Pistol Pete. When I was playing, at first I protested to my front office, who partially convinced me that it was a great thing to 'earn' a nickname.

"Eventually I came to realize 'if you can't beat 'em, join 'em.' By the time I got to San Francisco (with the Pioneers in 1981), they went full-blown, and we did promotional photos with a replica machine gun."

Hitting the big time

That same month that story appeared, Molly took the court for the first WBL All-Star Game. She'd made her initial splash just in time to earn a spot on the Midwest Division squad, and even though she saw limited playing time and didn't score, the experience helped open her eyes about the possibilities that lay ahead.

The game was played at the Felt Forum in New York, with the East squad overcoming an early 30-18 deficit to pull away for a convincing 112-99 win.

"I was thrilled to death, and my entire outlook on my pro career shifted," she recalls. "Even though I only played 4 minutes and maybe made one shot in that game, it was such an exciting experience to be there."

The trip back home from the game proved to be even more exciting — in Molly's words, "more excitement than I bargained for."

The plane left New York's La Guardia airport before dawn on the morning after the game, with the Iowa players exhausted

Tanya Crevier continues to perform at schools, churches, camps and halftime shows across the country.

from the trip. The plane took off, but then, "as we're up in the air, they're announcing there's a hydraulic problem and 'we don't know whether the wheels are up or down, so we're going to have to dump the gas over the ocean.'"

The flight crew announced they'd have to divert to JFK International, just 10 miles away, for an emergency landing on a foamed runway.

After the plane touched down, Tanya Crevier entertained the passengers and crew when they were held onboard for an nearly an hour, waiting to disembark: "I travel with my basketballs all of the time," she says.

"As this happened, I took a couple of my basketballs out of the bag and kept the people smilin' and happy in spite of the situation. Kept the 'enthusiasm' going!"

Once they finally left the plane, they had to go right back to where they'd started..

Molly continues the story: "Then, a few of us were put in a helicopter and flew over New York City back to La Guardia and saw the other All-Stars, who said, 'What are you doing here?' as we had left at 5:30 a.m., and we had a game in Minnesota that night. Fortunately, we were so exhausted we slept through most of the drama of the emergency landing and made it to our next game on time with some great stories for our Iowa teammates."

Meanwhile, Molly was busy acclimating herself to a new system under a new coach, who was hired just a week after her breakout 40-point game against Milwaukee.

Lein stepped down as interim head coach and installed Dan Moulton as his permanent replacement. Moulton, 33, had started the girls basketball and softball programs at Saydel High School in Des Moines nine years earlier, but had just been suspended for the second time during the season; his girls basketball team was 3-12 at the time. District administrators refused to disclose the reason for Moulton's suspension, but Lein backed Moulton: "I've investigated and think he was the victim of a personal vendetta in his high school job."

So, Moulton was in.

"Now we needed to learn a new system in midseason," Molly remembers, but Moulton still had her playing a reserve role most of the time: "Dan experimented with starting lineups, so I did start a few times in that stretch. However, Dan told me once that his grandmother told him I played better off the bench! Seriously."

Molly quickly became the team's top scorer, anyway, leading the Cornets by season's end with an average of 16.7 points a game despite several early games in which she barely scored anything. Doris Draving was right behind her at 15.6 points a game and led the team in rebounds with an average of 12.8. Robin Tucker, meanwhile, paced the team in assists at slightly more than six per game.

With the coaching situation often in disarray, Tucker also

contributed leadership when it was lacking from the bench.

"She had great court sense as to when to pass, shoot, or reset the offense, and we all trusted her," Molly says. "Fortunately, our team got along really well, and we did pull together when times got rough. But we only had like two basic offensive plays and nothing specifically for me to score. Sometimes in a tight game — both when Rod and Dan coached — we would be given instructions on the bench. As we walked onto the court, Robin would pull us together and say, 'That's never going to work, so let's do this,' and give us another play to run. And most of the time we would win following Robin's lead."

The Cornets were a streaky team under Moulton. A three-game winning streak starting Feb. 23 was bookended by a pair of impressive wins. It included a 50-point blowout of Dayton in which Iowa hit its highest point total of the season. Molly scored 35 as the Cornets cruised to a 131-81 win that avenged an overtime loss to the Rockettes in Moulton's first game. Then, after a 123-102 win over Minnesota, the Cornets handed the league leading Houston Angels a 96-94 setback March 4 in Des Moines. Molly scored eight of Iowa's last 11 points, including a pair of clinching free throws with 23 seconds to play

After that, however, the Cornets went into a four-game tailspin on the road that finally ended when they returned home for a 105-89 win over hapless Milwaukee. That kicked off a six-game winning streak — the first five at home followed by an easy win at Dayton — before the team closed out the regular season on the road against Chicago, holding a one-game lead over the Hustle for the division title.

Chicago built a 77-57 lead, but the Cornets cut the margin to one at 92-91 before falling short in a 98-96 loss. It didn't matter though: Since both teams finished the season with identical 21-13 records, they had to turn right around and meet again in the first round of the playoffs. The first game was scheduled for DePaul University, the Hustle's home court, with the other two slated for Ankeny High School, just north of Des Moines.

The location didn't sit well with the Hustle, which had expected to play in the Veterans Memorial Auditorium and complained to the league office about the arrangement. There was some dispute over whether the Vets Auditorium was available for the playoffs.

League president Bill Byrne said he'd been told it wasn't but had later found out otherwise. Lein said Byrne had misunderstood, and that it hadn't been available for the first game — which wound up being played in Chicago — but could have been secured for the April 12 and 14 games in Iowa.

Regardless, the Cornets saved a lot of money by playing at Ankeny, where Lein once coached, renting the gym there for just $300 a game compared to the $2,200 cost of renting the Vets. (The host team also got to keep all the profits from its home playoff dates.)

As a result of the Hustle's complaint, Byrne said he was looking into a policy prohibiting teams from playing in high school gyms during Season 2, and, indeed, the Cornets didn't play at any high school venues going forward.

They almost didn't play in the inaugural championship series, either: It took a major comeback in the third and deciding game to secure a victory over the Hustle, who were coached by Doug Bruno. Bruno had previously coached at DePaul University, and would return there as head women's basketball coach in 1988. As of this writing (2019), he still holds that position.

The Hustle lived up to their name with what Molly

describes as "a fast-paced run-and-gun game led by Rita Easterling and Janie Fincher." The team was one of the most popular in the league: Ten of its games were telecast on a local TV station, with each contest pulling in more than 140,000 viewers. The ratings were twice as high as the team had expected, and even better than they were for Chicago Black Hawks hockey.

"Their home games at DePaul always were so exciting to play in because back then, the full capacity was about 4,500 and their fans were loud and crazy, while the Cornets fans were a lot more conservative," Molly says. "Janie got her share of attention in Chicago, and fans loved to compare us and get photos of us together. We both had blond hair and played shooting guard and had posters — and that's where similarity ended." (More on those posters in a little while.)

The Cornets played a more deliberate style, centered on Molly's shooting, Tucker's playmaking and Doris Draving's rebounding. Draving had wreaked havoc on the boards with a club-record 25 rebounds to go with 26 points in a 115-101 victory over the Hustle at Evans Junior High in Ottumwa, just a few miles away from Molly's old home in Moravia. (Molly treated the crowd to a 15-point performance.)

The two teams had met six times in the regular season, with the Cornets winning four times and outscoring the Hustle by an average score of 109-103.

Two of the three playoff games would be even closer.

The Cornets traveled to Chicago for the first game, where they got a scare when guard Sister Green suffered was hit by a car while crossing the street and suffered a concussion. She was in the hospital for observation when the team played its postseason opener.

Iowa trailed by three points entering the fourth quarter but managed to force overtime before falling 112-107 despite Molly's game-high 30 points. Once again, however, Moulton chose to use her off the bench rather than start her.

He did the same thing again in the second game. With the Cornets back home and facing elimination, they built a 22-point lead in the third quarter on their way to a 114-101 victory April 12. That set up a third and deciding game two days later, again at Ankeny High.

In that final game, Iowa fell behind 30-12 after the first 10 minutes, committing 12 turnovers in the opening period. But the Cornets started a 16-2 run near the end of the first quarter to take their first lead at 38-36. Iowa trailed again by eight late in the third before rallying to take an 11-point lead with just over 2 minutes to play. Chicago was whistled for several fouls midway through the fourth quarter, and Coach Bruno was ejected after receiving his second technical.

The Hustle, however, came roaring back. The game ended bizarrely, after Molly scored the Cornets' last five points. Iowa led 118-115 with 1 second left and Fincher at the line for the Hustle; she would have three chances to make two free throws. (This rule, in effect in the NBA at the time, was also used in the WBL for shooting fouls committed when a team was in the bonus; the NBA eliminated the rule in 1981). Fincher missed the first free throw and made the second, leaving the Hustle two points down. She then threw the ball up hard, hoping to have it carom off the backboard into a teammate's hand, but it went through the net instead.

Connie Kunzmann successfully inbounded the ball to end the game and give Iowa a 118-117 win. Molly led the scoring with 28 points, while Draving added 21 points and 17 rebounds. The Cornets were on their way to the finals, where they would face the Houston Angels, the team with the league's best record.

"Houston was a lot more challenging," Molly says. "They were well-coached the entire season by Don Knodel and Greg Williams. Houston also had a tough backcourt with Belinda Candler and Paula Mayo."

In order to beat the Cornets, Williams knew the Angels would have to find a way to guard Molly, and he had a plan to do so. Her name was Karen Aulenbacher. And guarding Molly was so crucial that Aulenbacher would play all 48 minutes of the fifth and deciding game.

Aulenbacher had played at Baylor University from 1976 to '78, and would be inducted into the school's Hall of Fame two decades later. At Baylor, she had developed a reputation as "a tenacious and aggressive defender and the leading rebounder," and she built on that reputation in Houston.

"To play Iowa, you were going to have to slow Molly down," he says, "You weren't going to be able to stop her, but you had to make her work on every single offensive possession. We felt like we had the best perimeter defender in the league in Karen Aulenbacher: She was a very physical player, just a tough, hard-nosed competitor."

Molly still got her points, though. She wasn't in the starting lineup as the series tipped off, but she had 16 points in the opener, an 89-85 loss before a sparse crowd in Houston.

The next game, scheduled for two nights later, was rained out when a thunderstorm hit Texas at 5:30 p.m., cutting power and flooding city streets.

"We were there for the championship and we were staying at a hotel across the street from the Astrodome," where the game was being played, Molly remembers. "It rained and it rained until the water was up over the headlights of the car. It was like a biblical flood. So, they canceled the game and we had to fly back home and then catch another flight back to Houston" after the game was rescheduled.

Williams, meanwhile, recalls setting out for Astro Arena, the court adjacent to the Astrodome where the game was scheduled, and being unable to even get there.

"I got in my van and drove to the game," he says. "When I left the house, the water was already up over the curb. I came to Buffalo Speedway, and Kirby Drive, at one of the major intersections in Houston, and there was literally a river running down it. I got out of the van in my three-piece suit, and water was up to my knees. As I went forward, the water got deeper and deeper: It was almost up to my waist.

"I called Coach Knodel and told him, 'I can't get to the game.' He was already at the Astrodome, and he said, 'Yeah, the game's been canceled.'"

When the game finally *was* played, the Cornets wound up on the short end of another close one, letting a 73-67 lead slip away and falling to the Angels 102-98. The Cornets, however, found their rhythm as the series shifted back to Iowa, winning the next two games 110-101 and 89-79. Molly connected on seven consecutive long-range shots in the second quarter, when she scored 16 of her team-high 25 points to help Iowa even the series.

It all came down to one final game at the University of Houston, the only time the Angels played there all season, because they hadn't paid their bills at Astro Arena, and the Astrodome wouldn't allow the game to be played there.

Still, between 6,000 and 8,000 people showed up at Hofheinz Pavilion for the game. One of them was Del Harris, coach of the NBA's Houston Rockets at the time, who was in line to buy a ticket when Williams happened to catch sight of him and comp him a game pass. But Harris said, "No, I want to pay for a ticket. I want to support women's professional basketball."

When the game got under way, the Cornets struggled at the foul line and the Angels led most of the way. Molly hit a bucket to pull them within four at 64-60 in the third quarter, but then she and Draving each picked up their fifth personal foul. Despite this setback, Iowa kept it close and actually pulled ahead at 99-98 before Houston closed with a 13-6 run and claimed the title with a 111-104 victory. D.K. Thomas led the Cornets with 31 points, and Molly added 19.

At season's end, every one of the league's eight teams had lost money: Chicago had done the best, having shed "just" $150,000. But each of the eight teams had survived the season, even though the league had to bail out the Dayton Rockettes to the tune of $96,000. The league had even gotten some positive national exposure from no less a personage than Walter Cronkite, who featured it in a segment of *The CBS Evening News*.

"We haven't had too many bad things happen to us," founder Bill Byrne said, pointing out that "no sports league has ever made money in its first season."

Going forward, however, that was the goal.

To that end, on the same week that the championship series took place, owner George Nissen broke the news that the team was moving its headquarters from Des Moines to Cedar Rapids, where Nissen's business was located, so he could "have more input."

Lein, meanwhile, indicated that he wouldn't move with the team because of his own construction business interests. Moulton was also "looking into some other things."

One thing was clear: Big changes were afoot as the Cornets entered their second season.

5150 East Main Street
Columbus, Ohio 43213
614/868-8530
TWX-810/339-2434

July 21, 1978

Ms. Molly Bolin
400 S. Ryan
Colfax, IA   50054

Dear Molly:

Congratulations on being officially accepted as a member of the WBL
family. Your contract has been received, examined and approved.

We at League Headquarters want you to know that we are very proud of
you. Your selection by a WBL team is an indication to us that your
talents have been recognized by experienced player personnel directors
and scouts.

We hope that your career in the WBL - in addition to its historic ep-
isode in your life - will be a fruitful one, bringing not only fame
and self-satisfaction, but the gratification of knowing that you are a
pioneer in women's athletics.

If we can be of assistance to you at any time, please feel free to call
on us. Also, if you are ever in the Columbus area, we would be pleased
to have you visit us in the League Office.

Good Luck!

Bill Byrne
President

BB/mc

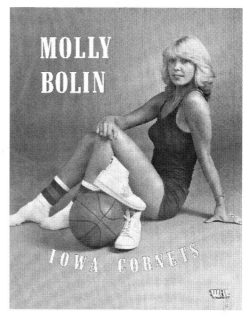

The two posters Molly produced during her second season with Iowa earned her extra money and the Cornets publicity.

Posters and Pistol Pete

One of the things that didn't change much in Molly's second year with Iowa was her pay.

Rod Lein was, indeed, no longer with the team when the Cornets came back for Season 2, and neither was Dan Moulton. Katie McEnroe, 25, moved over from the league office to take the reins as the new GM, while Steve Kirk assumed the coaching duties after a couple of seasons at Wisconsin-Eau Claire.

One of the first orders of business for McEnroe was re-signing the players from the first season, who had received one-year contracts. Molly was hoping for a significant raise, considering her status as Iowa's top scorer and her role in helping the team reach the finals. She'd set the league's single game-scoring record (twice!) and been named to the All-Star and All-Pro teams. There was also the matter of the team's move to Cedar Rapids, which meant Molly would have to move her family, as well.

But those hopes were quickly dashed.

"Our front office was much more focused on budget cuts than raising salaries," she says. "Katie was tough, and would not budge from her top offer of giving me an increase of $500 per month, even though I knew I was definitely on the low end of the scale compared to the rest of the league."

That $500 a month, spread over six months, wasn't really a raise at all, from Molly's perspective. It amounted to $3,000 — the same amount of money she'd made for being involved in a Hollywood movie prior to her first year with the team. Taking part in that movie had been part of the deal for players who signed with the Cornets. Owner George Nissen saw it as a way to promote his new team and the WBL as a whole. What he didn't see, when the filmmaker approached him about the project, was a box-office bomb in the making.

The silver screen

Michael DeGaetano was hardly a veteran Hollywood director. He'd made two previous movies — a space invasion flick called *UFO: Target Earth* in 1974 and a reincarnation-themed thriller called *Haunted* three years later. You can get an idea of how good (or not) these movies are by visiting the IMDb website. As of this writing, 301 viewers had given the first movie a rating of 2.4 stars out of 10, and the reviews for the second were only slightly better: 3.6 stars from a cross-section of 144 moviegoers.

Of course, that website didn't exist back in 1977, when DeGaetano approached the Cornets about making a film about a team of women's basketball players. His initial plan was to build the movie around the barnstorming All-American Red Heads team. DeGaetano wanted to get Detroit Pistons center Bob Lanier and Boston Celtics star John Havlicek for the film, and said he had Isabel Sanford from *The Jeffersons* TV sitcom lined up to play the team bus driver. Former *Laugh-In* regular Ruth Buzzi and *Eight Is Enough* star Dick Van Patten were also supposedly lined up to be in the movie.

None of them wound up making an appearance, and for whatever reason, the Red Heads didn't take part in the project, either. So, DeGaetano, 38, turned his attention to the Iowa Cornets. He'd planned to shoot his film in Des Moines from the beginning, so the new WBL team was a natural fit for the project — which he said he'd been thinking about for 15 years by the time he got ready to make it a reality. He even had a title for the movie: *Dribble.*

"Iowa girls basketball is serious, and the Iowa fans are proud of it — and should be," he said when he announced plans for the film in March of 1978. "Ours will be a comedy about a professional women's team."

When DeGaetano pitched the idea to Nissen about becoming involved in the picture, the response was enthusiastic. Not only would some of the team's players appear in the film, but Nissen agreed to put $1 million of his own money into the production costs.

"I just wanted to prove we could do something like this in Iowa," said Nissen, who revealed he'd bought out some of the movie's original investors. "People from Hollywood think it's about a $4 million project, but we did it for less because we did a lot of the work ourselves."

Nissen also may have thought he saw something of himself in an independent filmmaker who was standing behind his creative vision the same way Nissen had stood behind the trampoline.

"Another reason I decided to put money into the film is because I'm completely sold on DeGaetano," Nissen said. "He's a talented, dedicated man who is bucking the bureaucratic trend in Hollywood."

After *Dribble*, DeGaetano never made another movie. But at the time, it was such big news in Iowa that it took up a good chunk of space in the *Des Moines Tribune* article on the news of Molly's signing.

The plot focused on a women's team called the Vixens, whose coach takes all their money and leaves them stranded and broke. Befriended by a florist and his pothead son, they use the money from the sale of marijuana to finance the team. Still, they're about to be expelled from their home arena (called "Des Moines Arena" in the film), but in order to avoid that fate, they're given one last chance: They must win one of their next two games.

After losing to a women's team called the Omaha Beefeaters, the Vixens find themselves up against a men's team representing the Army and led by none other than "Pistol" Pete Maravich, who at the time was playing for the NBA's New Orleans Jazz and was the only recognizable name in a cast that also included 6-foot-4 actor Dennis Haysbert as a police lieutenant.

It was just Haysbert's third acting credit, following guest appearances on *Lou Grant* and *The White Shadow*, a basketball-themed TV drama. More than two decades after appearing in the film, he would become a regular on the series *24*, where he portrayed President David Palmer from 2001 to 2007. During the same period, he became a familiar face to other viewers by appearing in a series of commercials for Allstate Insurance. As of this writing, he had a total of 123 acting jobs to his credit.

Molly has one: in *Dribble*.

"After the big announcement of being the first player in the league, Rod Lein told me that part of joining the team would include a role in a movie that was going to be filmed that summer in Iowa," Molly remembers. "I don't know the entire story behind the scenes of how the movie director got in touch with the Cornets, but obviously Rod brokered a deal where our owner, George Nissen, financed the movie as a big publicity push for the Iowa Cornets *and* the new women's pro basketball league. I doubt either of them saw a script in advance, but part of the deal was that three of the Iowa Cornets would be main characters in the film and four would be hired actresses to make up the Vixens team, the main focus of the movie."

Lein was given discretion over which players he wanted to be in the movie, and Molly was the first person he told about it. He invited her over to his house to meet DeGaetano, and she was determined to make the most of the opportunity.

"I looked at this as a huge opportunity and possibly a big break, and it was so exciting," she says. "So, I dressed to impress and was pretty sure I could win him over, but what happened was exactly the opposite — the only thing he saw was that he already had an actress cast as the glamorous and busty dumb blonde player, and he didn't want anyone distracting from that character."

(The actress in question was Laurene Landon, a Toronto native making just her second film appearance. She had played high school basketball and, at 5-foot-9, was the same height as Molly.)

This put Lein in a bit of a fix, as he had already promised

Molly one of the main parts. But he promised her she'd still be involved in the movie and would be paid the same amount: $100 a day plus meals and the cost of a hotel room during the six weeks of filming. The total amounted to $3,000, more than half of what she'd be making for actually playing basketball during her first year with the Cornets.

"It was a blessing in disguise, as the Iowa players that were cast — Tanya Crevier, Robin Tucker, and Joan Uhl — turned out to be the best choices and my best friends," she says. "We had so much fun together, I was sharing a hotel room with Tanya."

Molly recalls "the pranks Tanya and I pulled on Robin and Joan — and they would retaliate and do something to us, or get our door open and throw us into the pool that was just outside the hotel room. Never a dull moment! Plus, I had a lot more freedom than anyone because I was working in different departments and the other girls had to be on set every day all day — moviemaking was a lot of sitting around waiting."

How good was Crevier? When she showed off her ballhandling skills to Maravich, he proclaimed, "I've never seen anyone that good." That was high praise coming from the man Hall of Fame forward John Havlicek once described as the best ball-handler of all time. In one movie scene, she did a trick shot in which she spun the ball on one finger, dropped it and used her knee to ricochet it off the backboard and through the net. The scene took just one take.

As for Molly, she got some screen time as a member of the fictional Omaha Beefeaters and got to work behind the scenes, working with props and as an assistant make-up artist. She also had another job: Finding marijuana to be used in the film. "One of my first jobs was driving back and forth with a truckload of marijuana that grew wild out there in Iowa," Molly says. "How we didn't get arrested is beyond me."

In addition, Molly put herself in charge of giving Maravich a ride to and from the set every day he was working on the movie: a total of about a week.

Cornets assistant coach Bruce Mason recalls the two of them hitting it off: "She talked with him about basketball a lot while we were shooting the movie," he remembers. "Their personalities were similar in that both had extreme confidence."

They were also similar in their scoring ability. Maravich, described by the Naismith Hall of Fame as "perhaps the greatest creative offensive talent in history," remains the all-time leading Division 1 scorer with an eye-popping average of 44.2 points a game during his time at LSU. During his 10 years in the NBA, he averaged 24.2 points a game and led the league in scoring for New Orleans during the 1976-77 season.

"Pete was very popular on set with the other male basketball players — most who were retired Division 1 players," Molly says. "He would perform tricks for the crowd during filming and would entertain while a shot was being set up and filming was on hold. He would hold court at meal times, large groups at his table, preaching about the importance of eating right, so he was always surrounded by people."

While there was chemistry between the two, neither of them acted on it.

"I wanted to hear all his stories and learn about pro basketball, as he was finishing his pro career and I was just starting mine," Molly says. "We had more deep conversations on our trips in the car alone, but both of us acknowledged right away that since we were both married, it would somehow cheapen our connection by acting on the attraction. I was far more interested in having a good friendship with him, and there was no shortage of attractive women around, no doubt, in his life as a basketball star.

"Though he made a big impact on my life, I never saw him or talked to him again after that, though I always hoped our paths would cross again — it just wasn't right to go out of my way to try to make it happen."

Unfortunately, not many people saw *Dribble*, either. It had a big premiere in Cedar Rapids, which the players attended — several of them dressed in tuxedos. But Molly bucked the trend, wearing a stylish red dress and fringed black cloak. Despite the lavish coming-out party, however, the film promptly disappeared from the radar, eventually resurfacing on VHS with a new title: *Scoring*. There were a number of sexual double-entendres in the film, which carried the taglines "These girls want to play ... with your funny bone!" and "A battle of the sexes: Who'll end up on top?" The risqué dialogue and the marijuana angle weren't exactly tailored to the tastes of Middle America.

"Mr. Nissen, who was a really conservative guy, was mortified when he saw the final cut of the movie," Molly says.

Still, Nissen publicly declared himself "satisfied" with the "light, fast-moving film" at its premiere, and Molly calls it "one of those B-movies that's so bad it's entertaining."

Doris Draving recalls it as "a poorly made joke of a film, but it was fun and exciting to be a part of. The director was basically robbing dear Mr. Nissen and producing a bomb of a movie. It is hard to even watch, as it was so poorly put together and the storyline not cool."

Its rating on IMDb is a mediocre 5.7 stars (still much better than either of DeGaetano's previous films), and the lone Amazon user to rate the film's VHS release gives it three stars out of five, with much of the review devoted not to the film itself but to praise for Crevier's ballhandling. The reviewer,

James H. Lister declares that "Tanya Crevier may very well be the greatest trick basketball handler who ever lived — even better than 'Pistol Pete' Maravich or any Harlem Globetrotter! The movie 'Scoring' is an indispensable basketball movie to see. Be sure you view it in order to see 'Pistol Pete' Maravich and dazzling Tanya Crevier."

Crevier could juggle four basketballs at once and keep six of them spinning simultaneously. She didn't see much court time for the Cornets, but Nissen was quick to recognize that her wizardry was a great way to put fans in the seats and keep them entertained during halftime.

"I shared my basketball show and my enthusiasm and inspiration at every school assembly, at every halftime show, at every basketball camp, at every civic club," she says. "It's my prayer I gave our Team and the WBL a positive image."

'Cornography'

Nissen and Lein had other ideas to promote the team, too. They got someone to dress up as a giant ear of corn, thus creating the team mascot they called Shucks. They purchased a bus, painted it in the team colors (green and gold) and dubbed it the "Corn Dog." And, in addition to Crevier, they hired a group of Polish acrobats to perform at halftime.

It was all part of building a buzz around the team that Nissen labeled "cornography."

"Traveling on our customized bus was fun, especially since many of our games were within a day drive, like Chicago, Milwaukee, St. Louis and Minnesota, and Dayton, the first year (and, of course, back and forth between Cedar Rapids and Des Moines — about 2 hours each way — for home games). It provided a chance for the team to really get to know each other and bond with all the time together.

"After games, the smaller players could sleep in the luggage racks that were carpeted, and others on the floor, also covered with new carpet. Some of us would take turns sitting by and talking to our bus driver — and team photographer and videographer — Everett Albaugh. He was awesome to have around."

Especially in the snow, which wasn't unusual in Iowa during the winter basketball season.

"Once when we got back to our cars in deep snow at 3 a.m., he worked hard to get my car started," Molly recalls. "He put gas on the carburetor, and flames shot up and singed off quite a bit of his permed hair. I never laughed so hard as I did when he looked in the mirror and checked to see what hair he had left — and the singed hair kept falling off."

One of her teammates, she remembers, had it even worse than she did: The wind blew the door of her soft-top Jeep open, and it wound up full of snow.

"Another time, there was a big snowstorm and we were trying to get back from Minnesota for a home game," Molly says. "We followed a snow plow practically the entire trip and ended up having to go straight to the gym to make it on time for our Sunday game. Nobody had their home uniforms, so we pulled our away uniforms from our bags that were under the bus and frozen solid with sweat — stood them up in the locker room to thaw out and made it out to the court just a few minutes late."

In fact, the Cornets had the misfortune of playing their inaugural season during one of the most brutal winters Iowa has ever seen. In Quad Cities, a couple of hours east of Des Moines, there was at least an inch of snow on the ground for 78 consecutive days, beginning just before New Year's and extending into mid-March. According to the National Weather

Service, January of 1979 broke records for snowfall and bitter cold in Quad Cities, where the temperatures averaged 6.3 degrees and dipped as low as 27 below on Jan. 2.

A record 18.4 inches of snow there fell from Jan. 12 to 14, and the snow was a record 28 inches deep for six days starting on the 14th, when the Cornets played Minnesota in Des Moines and lost a close one, 109-107. There's no record of how many fans braved the snows to make it to that game, but only 241 had showed up the previous night to see the Cornets top Chicago in Cedar Falls. It was the smallest home crowd ever to see one of their games.

Center Doris Draving recalls "getting stuck in a snowstorm all night and having to put on frozen, smelly uniforms on the bus and get off cold and hungry and play a game immediately. We lost to Minnesota, and our manager told us that 'good athletes would have adjusted to all that and won the game anyway.'"

Still, the team had to find ways to promote itself, and Molly played a key role in that.

"Mr. Nissen, who invented the trampoline, was a showman himself and loved watching the attention that Molly got and brought to our team," Cornets assistant coach Bruce Mason says. "Molly was always available for any promotion that we had and was a key factor in our success at the box office."

The promotions extended well beyond the confines of the arena. Promoting the league involved everything from doing interviews to "playing one-on-one with reporters just to get on the news," Molly says. "I wanted us to make it. I was all-in to make this thing work."

The players would appear in parades and go out into the community to hawk tickets. Molly recalls that Crevier "would put on music in a mall and spin that big ball, and crowds would gather around. We would run around handing out 2-for-1 tickets to our games."

Another time, Molly says, the team signed them up to do a similar 2-for-1 promotion at a grocery store. "The time we did it, of course, there was a big snowstorm. There was just one older woman in the store, and these girls in green outfits kept going up to her and asking, 'Do you want tickets to the Cornets game?'" The woman ended up walking away from them, stepping briskly up one aisle and down the next in an effort to avoid the eager Cornets.

From left, Mary Shrad, Rhonda Penquite, Molly and Connie Kunzmann wear the first-season wool road outfits in front of the team bus, also known as the "Corndog."

Those green outfits were part of the image, too, and the players were expected to wear them to promote the team on the road. Unfortunately, they weren't built for comfort.

"They were the ugliest things, and they were scratchy" because they were made of wool, Molly says. "But we had to wear them."

Clearly, something better was needed. That first season,

Robin Tucker stepped up and helped her teammates place a phone order for matching green satin Cornets jackets.

"They were customized with our names and uniform numbers sewn on," Molly recalls. "We got them delivered in time and were very happy to wear them instead of the green wool jacket to go to Milwaukee to watch the very first WBL game against the Chicago Hustle."

As for the green wool jackets, the team roasted some of them at a bonfire party at the end of the first season.

But even the new satin jackets almost got the team in trouble. On a trip to New York, the players wound up in a bad neighborhood, and police warned them they might want to change into something less flashy to avoid attracting the wrong kind of attention.

"Some of us sneaked out of the hotel to hop on a subway," Molly remembers. "We had never ridden one before and came out on the street in a bad area, and immediately the police came up and said, 'Do you have any idea where you are? Don't make my life difficult trying to protect you, so go right back where you came from.' We decided to take his advice after a quick look around."

Like members of the All-American Girls Pro Baseball League three decades earlier, the players were expected to set an example for their young fans.

"We weren't supposed to smoke or drink because they wanted us to be role models, which I didn't mind since I didn't smoke or drink anyway," Molly says.

Others did, though.

"I was married, and everyone wanted me to be their roommate because I would cover for them if they wanted to go out and party."

Poster pandemonium

The team's most successful promotion, however, was Molly's idea. When new GM Katie McEnroe offered her a $500 raise for the Cornets' second season, Molly pressed her for more: "The first season, I got an extra $3,000 by working on the movie, so I asked Katie how they would supplement my income this year, and she had no answer or no additional offer. She told me that for the Iowa Cornets to survive we could not go over budget, and that was the best she was able to do.

"So, I proposed an offer to her: I said I wanted to make and sell posters at our games for extra income and I wanted the team to pay for the photographer and the poster prints. She agreed, likely after finding out the low cost involved to make me happy."

Molly came up with the idea as her answer to Farrah Fawcett's iconic 1976 poster, which wound up selling more than 5 million copies. Fawcett parlayed the one-piece swimsuit pose into the best-selling poster of all time: It adorned the walls of many adolescent boys' bedrooms and made the actress more money than she earned for starring in *Charlie's Angels*.

"The whole poster idea stemmed from my admiration of Farrah Fawcett, who rocked the world with her million-plus-selling poster about 1976 — and you will see a similar pose in one of my posters," Molly says. "I read about what a huge seller it was and how much income that poster generated, and when I hit a brick wall with my contract negotiations to increase my salary, I was thinking outside of the box of ways to generate more income."

Molly's posters (there were two of them) might not have sold a million copies, but they did prove to be extremely popular: They sold out in multiple printings, even though —

unlike the Farrah prints — they were in black and white.

"Unfortunately, I didn't designate that I wanted *color* posters, so I ended up with the lower-cost black and white," she says. "As I remember, our printing costs were 50 cents each, and I sold them for $3 each. The first run was 500 prints, with 250 of each of the two poses. I believe that after the initial printing, I paid for the next two or three printings with my profits."

The posters caused something of a sensation. One featured her in a tank top and shorts with a basketball and a pair of sneakers, a half-smile on her face, in a pose obviously inspired by the Farrah poster. In the other, she was standing, in her basketball uniform, her body angled slightly toward the camera, her smile confident and her warm-up jacket slung over her shoulder like a superhero's cape.

The hero angle wasn't lost on a headline-writer at the *Des Moines Register*, who quipped, "Some athletes look like the Incredible Hulk; Thank goodness for Iowa's incredible Bolin!"

Another writer for the *Register*, columnist Chuck Offenburger, led off a piece in November of 1979 with the provocative question of whether the Iowa Cornets were sexist. Offenburger sought the answer with input from Nissen and McEnroe (although he didn't talk to Molly directly; she only made public comments about games, not about the team or the league.) The two tried to walk a fine line between the need to promote the Cornets and their dedication to the sport.

Nissen: "I don't think there's anything sexual about our promotions. But our players are good looking kids who play basketball, and I don't think it's wrong to point out they are not some kind of great big Amazons. Our advertising is a natural outgrowth of that. We're not selling the glamour girl thing. We're selling basketball. We're doing it in a personal sort of way because we've found that our fans like to relate to the players as persons."

McEnroe: "My main objective is to get people out to the games. We've been real pleased with our crowds in both Des Moines and Cedar Rapids. The advertising is working. We're not promoting games as freak shows, but we're also never going to deny our femininity. It's what makes us different from the NBA."

Offenburger never did reveal his own answer to the question of whether the Cornets were sexist, only concluding his column with the words: "Aw, to heck with sociology. Gimme a Molly Dolly poster."

It was Offenburger who came up with that nickname, much to Molly's chagrin.

"I always detested that name because I have a sister named Dolly — which I'm sure he didn't know!" she says.

Even though the posters were her idea, the league got behind her 100 percent. Molly kept the profits, while the Cornets benefited from the publicity. The posters helped put people in the seats which, as McEnroe had said, was her main objective, and that was Molly's goal, as well ... in addition to making extra money since the team wasn't willing to give her a bigger raise.

She "had to get people's butts in the seats," but that was just the first step. "I had to perform on the court" to keep them coming back.

"The team *and* the league backed me up," she says. "They loved all the attention it was getting. Most of the backlash was from some players from other teams and feminists who felt I was selling them out by promoting a sexy image rather than my basketball skills. Some even said I was allowing myself to be exploited by the men running our league."

Robin Tucker, the Cornets' point guard, observes: "Molly was perfect to promote an Iowa team. She was the hometown girl, scoring like crazy, and she was personable, attractive, always smiling. My favorite poster was the Machine Gun Molly poster" that came out when she was with San Francisco during her third season.

"Beyond her obvious good looks, Molly was a flash of blond hair and orange rainbows of shots," Dallas Diamonds executive Dave Almstead recalls. "Her poster was something every aspiring young girl wanted and she, who they wanted to emulate."

The Iowa posters were such a hit, she had some T-shirts printed up with a photo of her tossing a basketball in the air, and Cornet teammate Mary Schrad loved to tease her about making a shooting Molly Dolly — and still does to this day. That never happened, and the T-shirts only had a limited run because they cost a lot more to produce than the posters, and it was difficult to know which sizes to keep in stock. Only about 100 of them were made.

"Her posters were fun, sexy and well received," Doris Draving says. "Once we were stopped on the road between Des Moines and Ceder Rapids for speeding on our bus called the Corndog, and the policeman accepted her poster instead of giving us a speeding ticket!"

All this happened in the days before pro athletes were making millions of dollars from outside promotions. Ann Meyers of the New Jersey Gems, the league's biggest name, shot a 7-Up commercial. And Faye and Kaye Young, identical twins who played for the New York Stars, appeared in TV spots for Doublemint Gum for Dannon Yogurt. (The punchline was that the twins believed they liked different flavors of yogurt, but found out in the end that they both preferred blueberry.)

But both Meyers and the Young twins were playing in a major media center, New York City, while Molly was playing in the league's smallest market.

Molly did get paid $200 for endorsing Sport Shake and also appeared in a hot-tub commercial, but other than that, all she received was free equipment from Champion and adidas.

That was about the extent of it.

With this in mind, the posters were, in many ways, ahead of their time: a money-making campaign that predated the age when players like Michael Jordan and LeBron James made a mint from merchandising. During this period, in the late 1970s, even the NBA was struggling for exposure. Molly's tenure in the WBL came just before Magic Johnson and Larry Bird entered the men's league, bringing it the kind of attention the sport had never seen.

"With some good publicity in the Des Moines paper, my posters sold well at the games, and I received many fan letters through our office with checks included for a poster order," Molly says. "It was time-consuming doing the mail orders at home, but the front office helped me with sales during games. They would make sure the posters were delivered and picked up so I could focus on playing. I would get a check periodically from the sales at games, but I really didn't keep a close accounting of any of it."

"I really had no idea of the consequences, but as I became a star, the popularity of the posters went around the league, and next thing you knew, each team owner was looking for their own Molly Bolin to market the same way."

Chicago Hustle fan favorite Janie Fincher, for example, appeared in a poster wearing a red satin jacket and uniform shorts, with both hands in the air and "Janie," spelled out in sparkling letters between her arms.

"I thought it was *far* better than mine," says Molly, "but she took a lot of teasing for it."

Fincher, a 5-foot-7 shooting guard who averaged about 16 points a game in the league's second season, was so popular in the Windy City that, when the Hustle traded her to Washington, the resulting uproar forced the team to bring her back a month later.

But the first posters were Molly's idea, and in many ways, she became synonymous with them.

They were often the first thing people noticed about her — despite her impressive play on the court. In many quarters, she became known first as the blond poster girl rather than as the league's most prolific scorer. Even as late as 2018, a story on the Las Vegas Aces' WNBA website argued that "part of the reason for Bolin's emergence was her appearance." Such false assumptions lingered even though the posters didn't come out until the second season, by which time she had already set the single-game scoring record and made the all-league team.

"I do feel now that this controversy contributed to my accomplishments not being recognized after the WBL folded," Molly says. But, she adds, "I don't feel like I did anything 'wrong' and have no regrets. When you are new, you have to take everything you've got and go with it. The posters did get attention, but where we won the fans was on the basketball court."

Molly shoots over Brenda Chapman of the Milwaukee Does.

Molly strikes a similar pose in a family photo at age 2 and in a Southern California Breeze photo shoot at 22.

Molly with father Van, mother Wanda and younger brother Forrest

Moravia High School

Senior picture, left, and on the set of the movie *Dribble*

Molly, center, at the *Dribble* premiere

The Legend of Molly Bolin

Above: Molly, second from right, listens to interim coach Rod Lein during a team huddle in the WBL's first season. Also standing, from left: Tanya Crevier, Mary Schrad (mostly obscured), Joan Uhl, DK Thomas and Suzanne Alt.
Left: Molly drives for a layup for the Cornets.

Molly's first photo as a Cornet, above left; right, with Robin Tucker. Below: Cornet Connie Kunzmann plays a handheld electronic football game with Molly's first husband, Dennie.

Janie Fincher of the Chicago Hustle chats with Molly.

Above: Molly looks up at the referee, incredulous over a blocking call, after going down in a first-season game against the Chicago Hustle. Standing from left: Tesa Duckworth of Chicago (background); Robin Tucker; Nancy Rutter; Chicago's top scorer, Debra Waddy-Rossow; and Connie Kunzmann. Left: Pete Maravich with the "Army" team in *Dribble*.

Molly appears on brochures for the Southern California Breeze, left, and the Iowa Cornets, above.

The Legend of Molly Bolin

Above: Molly guards Donna Orender of the Chicago Hustle, who would later become president of the WNBA, while playing for the San Francisco Pioneers in the WBL's third season. At right, a publicity photo for the Southern California Breeze of the LPBA, which would later appear on the cover of a San Francisco newspaper.

Molly and the San Francisco Pioneers take on Nancy Lieberman, second from right, and the Dallas Diamonds during the WBL's third season.

Molly poses for a "Machine Gun Molly" photo shoot during the 1980-81 season; above, Molly watches from the sidelines.

Photo at left © Moulin Studios, used with permission

Molly with Lakers owner Jerry Buss, left, and Martina Navratilova

The Nancy Lieberman touring all-stars, front row: Rhonda Rompola, Tara Heiss, Janie Fincher, Suzanne Washington, Rita Easterling, Heidi Nestor. Back row: Molly, Carol Blazejowski, Joan Uhl, Cindy Noble, Nessie Harris, Nancy Lieberman.

Former WBL rivals Janie Fincher and Molly joined forces for the Nancy Lieberman tour.

Molly wore her USA all-star uniform and warm-up suit while conducting clinics after her playing career was over.

The Legend of Molly Bolin

Molly at the Hoosierdome in Indianapolis during a game between the
1984 U.S. Olympic Men's Team and a team of USA All-Stars. Molly and
the female stars played the women's Team USA earlier 67,000 people in
what was billed as "The World's Largest Indoor Basketball Game."

Molly stands beside the trophy case dedicated to her career at Moravia High School, above. At right, Molly joins fellow former WBL standouts Carol Blazejowski and Nancy Lieberman at the 2006 WNBA All-Star Game.

The Legend of Molly Bolin

Molly and family gather to support daughter Kenzie, No. 4, at her final college volleyball match.

Molly's warm-up suit on display at the Naismith Hall of Fame, left, and her personalized ball from her induction with the WBL Trailblazers at the Women's Basketball Hall of Fame in 2018, above

Top: Molly stands behind a sign celebrating Moravia's heritage. Above: Molly and John, back, with kids Michelle, Kenzie, Casey and Damien.

Janie Fincher, left, Molly and "Wicked" Wanda Szeremeta of the New Jersey Gems listen as league president Bill Byrne speaks about the WBL.

Most Valuable

WBL President Bill Byrne had big plans for the league's sophomore year. With the first-season championship series about to begin, he announced that the league would expand by adding several teams: New franchises had been approved for St. Louis, Dallas and San Francisco, giving the league a coast-to-coast footprint. In addition, the Dayton Rockettes — which the league had been operating since the ownership went belly-up in February — would be transferred to a group in Los Angeles.

"We'll announce Los Angeles and Seattle coming into the league before the playoffs end, and Boston is in for sure," Byrne said. We're working with people in Denver, but they probably won't be in until the 1980-81 season. We'll move to three divisions next season."

The WBL did, indeed, adopt a three-division format for its second season, but the "for sure" Boston entry never materialized, and the league never played in Seattle or Denver, either. Another city being considered, Indianapolis, disappeared from the conversation, as well. Instead, teams were added in Philadelphia (the Fox) and Washington (the Metros), but both ran into financial problems almost immediately and folded after just 10 games.

The Los Angeles team also failed to make it to season's end, disbanding three-quarters of the way through.

Back in Iowa, meanwhile, the Cornets prepared for their second season with a new general manager and a new head coach. Steve Kirk had coached men's college basketball at Northern Michigan University — where future Michigan State head coach Tom Izzo was among his players — and Wisconsin-Eau Claire before taking over the Cornets.

Kirk brought a different dynamic to the game.

"Steve Kirk brought discipline and structure to our team and a completely different system of playing," Molly says. "It could not be further from the freewheeling play of our first season. Kirk didn't believe in treating the women players any different from the men, and he thought we weren't tough enough. He encouraged us to get more and more physical on the court and rarely called any fouls, so we were literally beating each other up in every practice."

Kirk wanted to keep turnovers at a minimum, so he decreed that only certain players could bring the ball up court and designed a controlled fast break, "with each player knowing exactly when and where to fill the lanes," Molly says. He instituted a modern system of position play, giving each player a number, with 1 being the point guard, 2 the shooting guard, 5 the center, and so on.

As the designated 2 guard, it was Molly's job to get open shots.

"His system was the best ballhandler on the team was going to handle the ball and the best shooter was going to get most of the shots, and it held true," she says. "We all had our roles defined, and mine was to put points on the board, which I was more than happy to do."

But even though she'd set scoring records and been an all-league selection, she wasn't guaranteed a spot in the starting lineup. Before the season got under way, Molly says, he installed the team's No. 1 draft pick, Mo Eckroth from the University of Utah, as the starter at shooting guard, ahead of her.

"He was especially hard on me, often putting me in as second or third string so I would have to fight for a starting position," Molly recalls. "Even when I finally moved onto the first team just before the season started, he was harder on me than anyone else and almost never complimented me unless it was for defense."

When she asked him why he was so tough on her, he said he didn't want the rest of the Cornets to think he was showing her favoritism because she was getting all the media attention.

But Kirk's uber-serious approach wasn't limited to Molly — or to game time.

"We were always in trouble with Kirk on the bus," Molly recalls. "On a long road trip, even the day before a game we would be laughing and playing cards or dice, and he would come back and tell us to knock it off and put our game faces on and think about the game. But that only made things worse because we kept doing the same things only trying to be quiet, which was even more funny."

Molly started the season with a bang, scoring 38 points in a 124-86 rout of the newly minted California Dreams, connecting on all 10 of her free throws. But Kirk wasn't pleased with the

Cornets' performance, even though they forced 21 turnovers. His assessment: The team was relying too heavily on the fast break, wasn't "playing too smart" and needed to run the offense better.

Molly added 25 points in an 89-88 win over a Milwaukee team that featured the previous year's top scorer, Brenda Chapman, who had averaged 25.4 points a game. Then she upped the ante in her third game, scoring 44 points to win a showdown with Rita Easterling, the reigning league MVP, who had 35 for the Chicago Hustle as the Cornets prevailed 122-111.

Her 20 points in the last 14 minutes of a game against Washington sparked the Cornets' comeback from a 16-point deficit as they posted their fourth straight win to start the season.

Opponents were starting to figure out how quickly Molly could take charge of a game.

"Once opposing coaches and players became aware of what a big scoring threat Molly was, they devised ways to try and stop her by switching, putting a taller defender on her, or trying to not let her get the ball. At that point, she needed her teammates to help get her open," point guard Robin Tucker says.

Kirk, she says, "had great screening plays to free Molly up for shots.

"I remember one that we ran often had Molly line up on the left wing. As I brought the ball to the top of the key, Molly would get down screen from a post player to get open on the left wing; if not open, she got a back screen to go back door from the same post player; if (still) not open, she continued across the key and received a double screen from the right wing and the other post player as she exited the key and headed toward the right wing. So, basically, her defender was screened twice and then double screened by her teammates. If they switched defensively to cover Molly, that left her teammates open. She happened to have some pretty good teammates, too, by the way. We had to play man-to-man defense in the league — no zones were allowed — so the player guarding Molly was going to have a rough night."

Molly credits her teammates for helping her get open: "Charlotte Lewis at 6-2 could set mean picks for me. She called herself 'The Human Wall,' and she really was. Connie Kunzmann and Doris Draving were also great at setting screens to pick off the defense."

Molly had clearly taken her game up a notch from the previous season, when she averaged 16.7 points a game. She'd been the team's top scorer, but during her second season, she scored more points than that Season 1 average every single time she took the floor.

The Cornets kept on winning, and were the only unbeaten team left in the league by the time they dropped a 107-99 decision at Dallas in their seventh game. The Cornets won seven of their first eight games before they faced the one team they couldn't beat that season: the New Jersey Gems.

The Gems, led by Ann Meyers, won all three of their meetings with the Cornets during the season. When they rolled into Des Moines on Dec. 16, the Cornets had played four games in the previous five days and were, understandably, weary. But, at least in Molly's case, it didn't show.

Meyers performed up to expectations, racking up 29 points and 13 rebounds to lead New Jersey in a 108-100 win, but she wasn't the game's top scorer. That was Molly, who poured in 42 points on 14 of 21 from the field, including strings of five straight buckets in the third quarter and four more in the final stanza, when she scored 16 points.

Molly tallied 14 points in the third quarter and outscored

Meyers again in their second meeting, 34-19, but the Gems got the best of the Cornets a second time, pulling away for a 111-95 win. The Gems completed their season sweep in their third meeting, a 112-103 win at Elizabeth, N.J. When all was said and done, though, Molly had outscored Meyers in their three meetings 93-60, and the Cornets would make it to the league championship series, while the Gems missed the playoffs altogether.

Meyers, nonetheless, got more press.

"Because Molly did not play for a large university or a nationally ranked program before entering the WBL, she never got the respect or the awards that she deserved," Robin Tucker says.

Tucker recalls bumping into Meyers years later, after she had married Don Drysdale, the Hall of Fame pitcher for the Los Angeles Dodgers. (Meyers and Drysdale both became broadcasters after their playing days were over.)

"It had been many years since I last saw her, and I told her that I had played against her with the Iowa team in the WBL. She chuckled and said, 'Oh, you had Molly Bolin on your team. Did you ever get the ball?' I was stunned by that statement and said, 'I was the one calling the plays and giving her the ball!'"

Certainly, Molly's teammates weren't complaining.

"Molly was a team player and very humble about her ability," Tucker says. "Some players may have gotten really cocky, but not Molly. She was kind, caring, down to earth, and loved basketball. I remember Coach Nicodemus, our first coach, felt that when the game was on the line with seconds to go, having Molly come off a double-down screen to shoot what would now be a 3-pointer from the top of the key was a high-enough percentage shot to bet the game on.

"When Molly broke loose on one of her 50-plus point

games, her teammates had big smiles on their faces and were as happy about it as the hometown crowd. I don't remember having ever heard anyone on the team complaining that Molly shot too much or had the ball too much. Her strength was scoring: She could score, and we all knew it!"

The proof is in the stats.

In the 1979-80 season, she took more shots than anyone else in the history of women's pro basketball for a single season, but she also *made* more shots than anyone else in history. She hit more than 47 percent of her shots from the field that year. By way of comparison, over in the NBA that season, Pete Maravich was hitting 44 percent of his shots, Elvin Hayes was making 45.5 percent and Celtics rookie Larry Bird — who revolutionized the jump shot and weaponized it like never before — checked in at 48 percent.

Road to the playoffs

After the first game against the Gems, the Cornets hit a dead patch. Back-to-back games in Washington and Philly were canceled just before Christmas because those two teams had just folded, and that left the Cornets without a game for 11 days heading into a Dec. 27 road date with Liz "The Whiz" Silcott and the St. Louis Streak.

Silcott had led the University of British Columbia to a pair of Canadian national championships, but her erratic behavior led the Canadian National Team to kick her off the squad, not once but twice — the second time, right before the 1976 Olympics.

Silcott was 28 by the time she joined the Streak, but she soon made it clear she had plenty of talent, rocketing to the top of the league's scoring list.

Molly was right behind her.

When Silcott scored 50 points against the Minnesota Fillies (the same team Molly torched for 50 or more four times), she boosted her scoring average to 35.4 a game. She was averaging 32.7 — just ahead of Molly's 31-point average — by the time they were due to meet on the court for the first time. The media built the game up as a showdown between the league's two best scorers, and a crowd of nearly 3,000 fans turned out at Kiel Auditorium to see it.

Molly got the best of the head-to-head matchup, scoring 30 of her 42 points in the second half, while Silcott finished with 37. But the Streak won the game, topping the Cornets 115-109.

"The press created that rivalry — but being put in that position always brought out my competitiveness," Molly says. "Liz was a completely different player than me. Liz was more of a street-smart type player who could make moves while dribbling so you didn't know where she was going and could finish with her shot.'"

In a rematch between the two teams Feb. 7, the Cornets avenged their earlier loss 107-97, with Molly scoring 47 points to Silcott's 26.

But as good as Silcott was on the court, her problems continued off it, as she often refused to practice hard and clashed with her coach and teammates. The Streak traded her to San Francisco, where she finished the season with a 31-point scoring average. She was traded again after the season ended, to the Tampa Bay Sun — a franchise that had been approved for play starting in the league's third season but never got off the ground.

Silcott never played in the league again.

Molly, however, was just getting warmed up. She broke out of a mini-slump Jan. 8 with a 38-point effort in a 113-92 win over New Orleans that included a 30-foot jumper for three points at the buzzer to end the third quarter. (The league had added the 3-point shot for its second season.) Less than a week later, she broke her own scoring record with 54 points in Des Moines against Minnesota.

Plenty of fans were on hand to see it. The Cornets had scheduled some special promotions, and team's supporters responded: 4,418, showed up for the game at Veterans Memorial Auditorium, the second-largest home crowd in team history. The game was also televised on Des Moines TV station WOI, giving Molly an even bigger audience.

She didn't disappoint, hitting 22 of 35 shots from the field (63 percent) and 10 of 11 from the line. Twenty of her points came in the third period. But Molly almost didn't get the record, because Coach Kirk pulled her out with nearly 6 minutes left in the game. She had scored 48 points at that point.

"Kirk never hesitated to pull me from a game if I did anything wrong," Molly says. "When I was a few points from setting the record, he sat me down for not running the right offense."

Kirk later said he was concerned that Minnesota might mount a comeback — even though the Cornets led by 21 points at the time. He put her back in a minute and a half later, after assistant coach Mason shouted to get Kirk's attention and let him know she was close to the record. ("I would have put her back in, anyway," Kirk later insisted.)

Molly had 4 minutes and 20 seconds left to break the record, but she barely needed half that, sinking a 15-foot jumper from the left side with 2:06 remaining — which prompted Kirk to pull her out for the final time. When the final horn sounded, fans from all over the arena converged on the court to congratulate her, waving papers and seeking autographs.

Molly, however, was more concerned about one fan who

remained in the bleachers: "At the end of the game, I was mobbed by the fans, but my mom passed out in the stands" from all the excitement, she recalls. "I thought she had died."

Wanda Van Benthuysen was fine, it turned out.

Games like her record-breaking performance against Minnesota helped Molly earn her second All-Star nod in as many years, joining teammate Doris Draving on a squad to be coached by Kirk. Molly was the high scorer for the West with 25 points in a 115-112 victory.

But the Cornets found themselves in a dogfight with Minnesota for the top spot in the Midwest Division during the second half of the season. With six games left for the Cornets, the Fillies held a two-game lead on Iowa and were four games ahead in the loss column. But the Cornets were able to cut that lead in half, as Molly scored 32 points in a 102-76 rout of Milwaukee, while Chicago posted a 112-95 win over Minnesota.

That set up a March 2 showdown with the Fillies in Des Moines, with the Cornets poised to move into a tie for the division lead with a win. Playing before nearly 3,500 fans, Molly rose to the occasion, once again eclipsing her own single-game scoring record. It was in this game Molly fell to the floor with an injured shoulder in the second quarter ... and recovered to score what remains a record for the most points in a single women's major pro basketball game: 55. (For those keeping score, Elizabeth Cambage of the Dallas Wings set the WNBA record in 2018 with 53 — equaling Molly's third-highest total.)

With that effort, Molly surpassed Silcott as the league's leading scorer. The Cornets not only beat the Fillies, they demolished them 125-85 in the second of what would become six consecutive wins to close the season. On March 9, Molly scored 40 points as the Cornets took a two-game lead over the

Fillies with a 101-81 rout of St. Louis. And she closed the regular season a week later with 36 points in a 106-73 romp at Milwaukee that turned out to be the Does' final game.

She finished the season with 1,179 points scored, a record for women's pro basketball that still stands, scoring 40 points or more eight times and averaging 32.8, another enduring standard.

"The second year of the league, when Molly went on those 50-point scoring sprees, I was telling everyone that she had radar," Robin Tucker recalls. "Everything was going in. At times, she would pull up so quickly that her hair would be across her face completely blocking her vision as she let it go and the ball would still go in! It was on those days that her teammates smiled the most."

The only other player to score more than 1,000 points in a season was Carol Blazejowski, who edged out Molly for the league scoring title in the WBL's third season.

No one has done it since.

In all, six of the top nine single-season point totals for women's pro basketball belong to WBL players.

50-point games in women's pro basketball, 2019				
Pts.	Player	Opponent	Score	Date
55	*Molly Bolin, Iowa (WBL)* *	Minnesota	125-85	3-2-80
54	*Molly Bolin, Iowa (WBL)*	Minnesota	109-93	1-13-80
53	*Molly Bolin, Iowa (WBL)*	Minnesota	126-109	3-27-79
53	Carol Blazejowski, N.J. (WBL)	Minnesota	118-113	3-13-81
53	Liz Cambage, Dallas (WNBA) *	New York	104-87	6-22-14
51	Riquna Williams, Tulsa (WNBA)	San Antonio	98-65	9-8-13
50	*Molly Bolin, Iowa (WBL)* **	Minnesota	128-111	3-29-80
50	Liz Silcott, St. Louis (WBL)	Minnesota	93-90	12-19-79

* League record
** Playoff record

Back to the finals

The Cornets, meanwhile, closed out their schedule at 24-12, one game ahead of the Fillies, and secured a bye in the first round of the six-team playoffs. But they hadn't seen the last of Minnesota, which also qualified for the playoffs and earned the right to a semifinal rematch with Iowa by dispatching New Orleans 2-1 in a best-of-3 series.

After dropping the first game of the series, the Cornets came back to win the next two — and their second straight trip to the finals. They won the second behind Molly's third 50-point effort against them in the space of 2½ months: She had 35 by halftime and hit 18 of her 19 shots from the field. The Cornets then won the third and deciding game as Molly scored 25 in a 95-92 nail-biter.

Their opponent in the finals: the New York Stars, coached by former Knicks guard Dean Meminger.

The Stars had the best record in the league and had dispatched San Francisco in two straight games to win their semifinal series. Their dominance continued in Game 1 of their series with the Cornets, who fell behind 91-77 near the start of the fourth quarter, then got buried as New York scored 16 straight points and pulled away to a 128-96 victory. It didn't help that Molly sat out the final period with an injury.

"I don't know what happened, but our first two playoff games in New York were terrible, including the coaching," she recalls. "It felt like nobody was ready to play or wanted to win. The first game we lost by about 30. I had 31 by the third quarter but sprained my ankle and sat out — not by choice — the rest of the game as we got stomped and the Cornets couldn't seem to score."

The trip to New York wasn't without its high points,

though. It was near the end of the disco era, and a nightclub at 254 West 54th Street in Manhattan seemed like the center of the universe, drawing celebrities like Farah Fawcett, Ryan O'Neal, Bianca Jagger and Diana Ross.

And, for an ever-so-brief moment, Molly Bolin, who ventured out to Studio 54 during the Cornets' trip to New York with teammate Pat Hodgson.

It wasn't easy to get inside. Nile Rodgers and Bernard Edwards of Chic were once denied entry to the club, even though they'd been invited by Grace Jones. (The experience inspired them to compose the hit *Le Freak*, which started out as an expletive-laced response to the experience.)

Molly had slightly better luck.

"We had met a couple of guys who said they get picked to go in all the time, so we stood in the freezing cold outside of the velvet ropes and waited," she says. "Possibly because of our green satin jackets, Pat and I were soon motioned forward, and they let us in past the ropes. When we realized the cover charge was $20 each — which we didn't have — we went back out and tried to get them to let the two guys in. Next thing we knew, Pat and I got pushed back outside the ropes. At that point, we decided to catch a cab and go back to the hotel. But it was still a fun adventure."

As it turned out, Molly and Pat weren't the only two members of the Iowa group out late that night. When they got back to the hotel at 2 a.m., they had to "dive behind some pillars" in the lobby when they saw Coach Kirk talking to a woman there.

So much for curfew, coach.

Unfortunately, the series wasn't nearly as much fun for the Cornets. The second game wasn't any better than the first: The two teams were competitive at the outset, with the Stars leading

23-21 heading into the second period. But Molly didn't play either of the next two quarters, and by the time the fourth period got under way, New York led 82-69.

The Stars used a full-court press to force 42 turnovers and won going away, 119-99. Molly finished with just 19 points, almost 14 below her average, but was on a pace to exceed it had she played all four quarters.

"In Game 2, Kirk benched me all of the second and third quarters 'for playing poor defense,' and we lost by 20. I scored 19 points in the two quarters I played. It almost felt like he didn't want to win and gave up way too early in both games. ... It was no wonder I was not letting it happen at Grand View in Game 3."

Grand View was, of course, the site of Molly's collegiate triumphs, and she would need another if the Cornets were to avoid elimination in the best-of-5 series. It was the first time Iowa had ever played a game there, and a sellout crowd arrived to root on the home team.

"Dean Meminger walked over to me as I was stretching near the sidelines and attempted to get in my head," Molly recalls. "I had heard he pretended to be me in their practice and they worked on preventing me from getting the ball. He said, 'We are shutting you down and closing out the series tonight.' I said, 'Well that's not going to happen. Do you know where you are? This is my house!'"

That response was typical of Molly's competitive spirit.

"Molly was a fierce competitor and was an extremely confident player," Bruce Mason says. "One of my favorite stories that I have told many times was about Molly. We were playing a game in the WBL and Molly had missed about five shots in a row and we called a timeout. When Molly came to the huddle she was smiling, and I said, 'What's so funny?' Molly said that she had missed the last five shots she would probably make the next five. That 'state of mind' confidence, is what I have told many shooters that they need to have to be successful."

Molly translated into that confidence into a huge game that saved the Cornets from elimination against the Stars. She poured in 49 points — including 30 in the second half — finishing just one point shy of the playoff record she'd set a few days earlier against Minnesota.

Molly scored 15 points in the third quarter and hit two free throws to give the Cornets a 100-83 lead with 11:02 left in the game. But the Stars rallied to pull within a basket at 113-111 before Molly sandwiched a pair of baskets around a New York free throw to put the game away. Charlotte Lewis' basket with 5 seconds left closed out the scoring, as the Cornets won 119-112.

"I was familiar with the baskets" at Grand View, Molly said after the game. "I had a feeling I was going to hit well."

For Game 4, the series shifted to Cedar Rapids, where the Cornets hadn't lost in their last 15 games, stretching back over two seasons. But before they even got there, the team got some bad news: Kirk had benched center Doris Draving, the league's top rebounder, and forward Pat Hodgson, neither of whom would start as punishment for failing to ride the team bus back to Cedar Rapids after Monday's game.

"That is a rule we have had all season," Kirk said. "It might be a rinky-dink rule, but we abide by it. This is a poor time of the season to start taking people out of the lineup."

Draving had pulled down 18 rebounds in the win at Grand View, and the pair had combined for 29 of the Cornets' points. But Kirk held firm: Charlotte Lewis would get the start in place of Draving, while D.K. Thomas would replace Hodgson in the lineup.

Hodgson and Draving both entered the game before the first quarter was halfway done, and Iowa was more than competitive most of the way after a torrid first quarter ended with the teams tied at 36. The Cornets led at halftime, then scored the first six points of the third quarter to go up 73-61, but ultimately ran out of gas.

The game was tied again at 98 with less than 10 minutes left; then the Stars went on a 13-2 run and never trailed again, scoring the final six points to seal a 125-114 win and claim the title.

Molly led all scorers with 36 points.

MVP with a catch

After the season, Molly, Janie Fincher and some other players took part in a promotional tour Bill Byrne put together to test potential markets for other teams. The tour, which pitted a team of WBL stars against college all-stars, brought her together with Meminger, whose Stars had just defeated Iowa for the title.

Molly doesn't remember much about the tour, but she does recall sitting next to Meminger and discussing the league's future, based on what he'd heard from the league office: "We talked about the likelihood that neither the Cornets nor the New York Stars would return for the third season."

That likelihood would become reality next fall, and it couldn't have surprised anyone who had knew about Iowa's struggles in finding an owner to succeed George Nissen or the amount of money the Stars were paying to rent Madison Square Garden — while drawing crowds that could charitably be called sparse. (In fact, the smallest crowd to see a Cornets game in their second season turned out at the Garden to see them play the Stars in January: Just 679 fans showed up to see New York improve its record to 12-2 with a 109-101 win over Iowa.)

But Meminger had other news for Molly, as well.

"Dean also told me that I had to keep it a secret until announced, but he was present when the word came in that I was voted as the second-season WBL MVP," she recalls. "I don't know any details of who voted, but I'm guessing league coaches and/or owners."

That shouldn't have come as any surprise, either. The real surprise came after the tour was over, when she heard a different story about the award from a reporter who called to get her reaction.

"I remember being in Moravia when a call came in from a reporter who had tracked me down and wanted to know how I felt about being selected as the *co*-MVP with Ann Meyers. I was caught by surprise and stumbled through the interview the best I could. But my next call was to Bill Byrne. I was really upset that nobody bothered to 'officially inform me' — and I hadn't heard anything about Annie also being *co*-MVP — and my first call came from a reporter!

"Bill told me that the league had just announced it and the reporter just beat him to the call. He told me that being *co*-MVP with Annie was going to be the best thing to ever happen to me and her name recognition was crucial for the league.

"Now I had — and still do — nothing but the utmost respect for her as a player, as Annie finished in the top five of almost every stat category in the league while playing for the New Jersey Gems. But I told Bill that while he believed Annie's name helped the league, I didn't see how it helped me at all."

Looking back, though, she says Byrne might have been right: "I probably received more public credibility being linked with her."

She didn't get anything else, though. Byrne ended up being removed as commissioner later that summer, and she never received a trophy or even so much as a certificate acknowledging the award.

Soon, she wouldn't have a team in the WBL, either. In fact, she was bound for a whole new league.

Second-season Cornets. Front: Robin Tucker, Molly, DK Thomas, Nancy Wellen, Sister Green, Tanya Crevier. Back: Team assistant (name not available), Rhonda Penquite, Pat Hodgson, Connie Kunzmann, Charlotte Lewis, Doris Draving, Nancy Rutter, Mo Eckroth, Denise Sharps, Steve Kirk (head coach), Bruce Mason (assistant).

Molly speaks to a reporter after scoring 54 points against the Minnesota Fillies to break her own single-game record.

Pacific Pioneer

Cracks had started to show during the WBL's second year: Three teams (Philadelphia, Washington and California) had failed to complete the season, but Byrne had plans to expand and fill the void and offered assurances that some of the league's struggling franchises were in good shape. "The Milwaukee franchise is super now," he said in April, just after the second season concluded. "Dallas and Houston are in good shape. There will be a team in Los Angeles."

Byrne himself owned a new franchise in Tampa Bay called the Sun, and talks were under way with potential owners in Jackson (Miss.), Denver, Seattle, Portland and San Diego. Byrne said there would be a minimum of 13 teams in the league for Season 3, with possibly as many as 16.

Dallas was, in fact, in good shape — at least good enough to play in the league's third year — but that was about the only thing Byrne said that turned out to be accurate. The Tampa Bay team never got off the ground, and none of the other five potential expansion cities joined the league. One of two new teams, the New England Gulls, would last just 12 games before folding; the other, the one originally set to play in Denver, moved to Omaha before the season even started because it couldn't find a place to play in Colorado.

As for Milwaukee, the team's general manager, Gene DeLisle, had taken a job with the new Ladies Professional Basketball Association. The Does changed their name to the Express but never played another game. So much for being in "super" shape. But even worse, every one of the three franchises that had competed in the league's first two championship series also disbanded. They had also been the three division winners from the second season: the Cornets, New York Stars and Houston Angels.

In Houston, there had been a glimmer of hope early in the second season when news broke that the Angels had been sold for $1 million. But it turned out to be a false report, and the team was forced to soldier on with little or no money in the bank. The coaches' paychecks bounced right before Christmas, and the players weren't getting paid, either. It got so bad the coaches told them they didn't have to practice, and it was up to them whether they suited up for games.

When it came time to take a 7 o'clock flight to the West Coast for a game in San Francisco, assistant coach Greg Williams told his players: "If five of you show up at the airport to go to San Francisco, we'll go and play the game." He didn't know whether any of them would.

As it turned out, all eight players from the previous year

showed up; the only no-show, Williams says, was a draft choice who was never heard from again. But since the coaches didn't feel right asking the players to practice without pay, the rusty Angels lost eight of their nine games to start the new year. The team's owners weren't pleased, but the coaches couldn't reveal *why* the team was playing so poorly.

"We couldn't tell them that all we were doing was just playing games," Williams says. "We didn't feel like we could ask them to practice when they weren't being paid — they didn't get any paychecks in January."

Even though they were 18-6 outside of that one bad stretch and won their division by 2½ games, the Angels failed to make a repeat trip to the finals, bowing to divisional rival San Francisco in the best-of-3 first round. The third and deciding game of that series was the last one they ever played, as the franchise folded at season's end.

Cornets come undone

At the start of the second season, the Cornets had looked to be in better shape, financially, than the Angels or most of the other WBL clubs. Nissen was well monetized and committed to the team. The team was also at the height of its popularity: "The Cornets' crowd attendance and team success was one of the best in the league — we weren't selling out 17,000 seats, but we had great media coverage and the popularity was growing, especially as we reached out to the schools around the state," Molly remembers.

But it was 1979, the year of the Islamic Revolution in Iran, where Nissen had been heavily invested in business dealings with the nation's leader, the Shah. His company had shipped $6 million worth of athletic equipment to the country, but the Shah was deposed before Nissen received any money for it.

He lost the entire sum. That, on top of his ill-fated $1 million investment in *Dribble* the first season, left him too cash-poor to continue running the Cornets. He sold 60 percent of the team in January to a former deejay named Dick Vance, retaining a 20 percent stake himself, while former GM Rod Lein purchased another 20 percent. In the midst of it all, the players made whatever sacrifices they could to keep the team afloat through the end of that second year. Vance, 53, hoped to make the Cornets a staple of a cable TV station he owned in Des Moines.

"We hope to create new fans through television," he said at the time.

But Vance sold 9 percent interest in the team to a restaurateur named Guy Falbo. Then, just two months after he bought the majority stake, he turned it back over to Nissen — who said a check Vance had written to him had bounced. Checks dated March 1 to Molly, Connie Kunzmann, Sister Green, Robin Tucker and assistant coach Bruce Mason also failed to clear, although they were later paid.

Meanwhile, Vance ran into trouble with the state attorney general when 270 people who had purchased vacations on one of his cable TV shows said the trips were canceled. According to a report at the time, a check to the Florida travel agency booking the trips had bounced.

"Dick Vance was in the news for not providing vacations people bought, and people interviewed on TV said, 'Well, I bought a vacation and didn't get it and Vance owns the Iowa Cornets team, so now I might own one of the Cornets, but I'm not sure which one!' We were laughing after seeing this while wondering if it could be true! Robin was the first one to smell a rat at the press conference introducing Vance as the Cornets new owner — she told us there was something 'cheap' about him and didn't trust him."

A Des Moines travel agency sued Vance for $7,524, and Mason would sue Vance and Lein two years later, demanding more than $6,000 in back pay and expenses.

The team, meanwhile, tried to weather the storm. "We said, 'We can pack our own lunches. We don't have to stay in a hotel; we'll just drive there and drive back'" on day trips to road games, Molly says. "But then we just kept winning," prolonging the season into the playoffs and, eventually, all the way to the finals.

Draving adds: "We called ourselves the 'Poornets' as we could barely afford groceries as the salaries were so meager. They gave us 25 dollars a day to eat breakfast, lunch and dinner. In my three years of giving it all I had, I made a total of $27,000 before taxes. I am now crippled from so many ankle injuries."

By the end of the season, the Cornets' future was in doubt, to put it mildly.

"After our loss to New York in Game 4 of the WBL Championship, the team held an awards banquet and assured us all that new ownership and financial support was forthcoming for Year 3 and to hang tight," Molly recalls.

One positive sign: The team took part in the league draft, selecting All-American point guard Holly Warlick of Tennessee.

But there were plenty of negatives. Steve Kirk, who lived with his wife and three children in Cedar Rapids, nonetheless quit in early July because he hadn't been paid since May 15. He found a new job one state over as head coach of the expansion Nebraska Wranglers, which he considered more stable than the Cornets even though the Wranglers were owned by the same man whose California Dreams had folded before the end of their only season.

"I wanted to stay here to begin with, but I got tired of waiting" Kirk told the Associated Press. The Cornets management, he said, "told me they would have something together May 1. Then it was June 1. Then it was by the (June 16) draft. I still don't see anything. I've got some responsibilities to take care of." In other words, he needed money to support his family.

Assistant coach Bruce Mason also left, taking an assistant's post at Drake.

Despite the departures, Lein remained optimistic, saying there was a 75 percent chance the Cornets would live to see a third season. He said he had six of the 10 investors in place to make it happen. But in August, Lein himself resigned, leaving Nissen in charge once again.

On Aug. 20, he hired Zeke Hogeland as the team's new coach and general manager. Hogeland, 54, had coached the University of Northern Iowa men's team from 1967 to 1974, but he'd never coached a women's team and, at the time of his hiring, was working as a golf course and bowling alley operator.

"We were told that a new coach was hired for the Cornets, but they wouldn't negotiate any contracts until the team finances were secured," Molly says. "When I actually met with the coach, I was very unimpressed, as he couldn't or wouldn't answer any of my questions about what was really going on with the team."

California or bust!

By early September, leading rebounder Doris Draving had signed with the Tucson Storm of the new Ladies Professional Basketball Association as that team's top draft pick, while guard

Robin Tucker had jumped ship to the LPBA's Albuquerque franchise, the New Mexico Energee.

The LPBA was courting Molly, too. The same *Des Moines Tribune* story that broke the news of her teammates' departure reported that she'd been to the West Coast twice for talks with the league's Southern California Breeze.

Other teams were lined up were the Oakland Oaklanders (or Outlaws), San Jose Chips and Phoenix Flames. A team planned for Las Vegas never materialized.

The league hoped to succeed where the WBL was faltering by playing its games in low-rent venues like high school gyms and municipal auditoriums rather than marquee arenas like Madison Square Garden and the Astrodome, where small crowds and high rents had combined to doom the New York Stars and Houston Angels. The LPBA sought to save on travel costs, as well, by creating a regional league rather than trying to play from coast to coast.

Tony Mercurio, general manager of the Breeze, said at the time that the league's "manual for success is simple: We simply have to do the opposite of practically everything the Women's Pro Basketball League did." That included not expanding too quickly, as he said the WBL had, and doing things differently in Southern California, where he was convinced the Breeze would succeed where the California Dreams had failed. He said the league paid its bills on time and in cash.

But despite this goal of fiscal prudence, one thing the league wasn't skimping on was salaries. Draving said she'd signed with Tucson for more than twice what she'd made with the Cornets, and Molly was being offered a significant raise, as well.

"I began receiving phone calls from Tony Mercurio all summer, who was the general manager for the Southern

California Breeze," she says. "He actually flew me out to California two or three times to show me what he could of the office and organization and go to Disneyland — my first time going."

"I was offered $30,000 to go to the new league and all kinds of incentives and bonuses for performance." (In all, there were 40 specific incentives that could allow her to make as much as $20,000 more.) "Even though I knew I wouldn't receive that if the league didn't make it, it still was my best offer on the table that summer."

Mercurio says he wouldn't even have stayed involved if he hadn't been able to sign Molly.

She was *the* marquee player, not just for the Breeze, but for the entire league.

"I wanted to help start the league, but I wouldn't have gone through with it unless I had signed Molly Bolin," Mercurio says today. "I wanted her because the league needed points, scoring. There was no better women's player in the country that can deliver scoring better than Molly. I tried to sign others, but Molly took most of what I had for salaries. She was worth it: a great scorer who brought credibility to the league. Unfortunately, I threw away a lot of money, and I would never do that again."

Naturally, the WBL didn't take too kindly to Molly's negotiations in California.

"As word got out about who I was talking to, the heat got turned way up," she says. "Bill (Byrne) would call and threaten me not to leave the WBL or I could face legal troubles. I also began to get calls from other WBL owners who wanted me to go there. Iowa had not yet officially folded, and the scramble was on to grab players."

In addition to the Cornets, the New York Stars and Tampa

Bay Sun tried to convince Molly to join their rosters, but neither of those teams would play a single game in the third season.

When she signed with the Breeze in late September, Molly not only agreed to play but to serve as the team's assistant coach. She brought Tanya Crevier and Joan Uhl with her, but losing Molly was the biggest blow for the Cornets. The lead paragraph in the *Des Moines Register*'s story on the news of her new contract put it succinctly: "The death knell may have sounded" for the Cornets. And five days later, it was official: Nissen put the franchise on hiatus for the 1980-81 season, and it would never play a game again.

Nissen had hoped to bring the team back the following season, which ultimately was never played, and wanted Molly to return and play for the Cornets after sitting out a year: "I think mainly they were counting on our loyalty to the team and our lack of getting professional advice from an agent or a lawyer," she recalls. "Even as young as I was then, having a team let you go for a year then being obligated to go back didn't make any sense."

The loss of the Cornets, the league's first franchise, was a major blow to the WBL.

"I was surprised and brokenhearted when the Cornets folded," Doris Draving says. "That really was the main breaking point for the whole league, as we were considered the strongest link in the chain. I thought we had made it after two years, but no."

So, as her old team called it quits, Molly headed to California, where she would be serving as an assistant to Australian basketball legend Ken Cole. Still, despite her title, she admits she did "absolutely zero coaching on that team." That was Cole's department, and he was, in Molly's words, "light years away from what I was used to as a coach."

Cole had plenty of experience. He'd played for the Australian national team in the 1964 Olympics and had won two national titles in six years of coaching women's basketball. Mercurio had rented her a condo in Santa Ana, not far from the Breeze team offices, and set up a string of promotional appearances for her. In a new outdoor photo shoot, she remade her image to look less Midwest conservative and fit in more with the Southern California beach culture.

It was a great time to be involved in basketball, especially in Los Angeles. The Lakers had just won their first NBA title in eight years, sparked by a rookie guard named Magic Johnson who had ushered in the Showtime era and, together with Boston's Larry Bird, a new era of heightened popularity for the league.

Greg Williams sent Molly a bumper sticker that read "MAGIC & MOLLY: NO PLACE LIKE HOLLYWOOD," and Molly attended a press conference at the Lakers' arena, the Forum in Inglewood.

"Magic Johnson was the star of the day, and I was given a short time on the schedule to announce the new women's pro basketball team," Molly says. "But when I inadvertently got skipped in the program, Magic called me up to the podium that turned into an impromptu interview in front of the press, as he was genuinely interested and asked great questions."

It wasn't her last contact with the Lakers. Team owner Jerry Buss would later invite her to a pregame dinner at the Forum Club and to watch the Lakers play from his private box.

"There was always a group of about 12 to 15 guests that consisted of celebrities from both sports and entertainment," she says. "Once Sugar Ray Leonard, at the height of his fame, was there with Ola Ray, the girl who starred in Michael Jackson's *Thriller* video. There was a private lounge we went to after the game where most of the players would come in, and I would see rock stars sitting at the bar. Of course, everything was free — food and drinks — but your name had to be on the VIP list or be in Jerry's group to get into that private area.

"I did attend (Lakers) games fairly often in those days and only had to call to request a ticket. I remember at the Lakers postseason playoff games, the excitement was ramped up so much more than in the regular season that you could literally feel the electricity in the air!"

But while Molly was enjoying her introduction to Southern California, it put a strain on her marriage.

"I was pretty happy to be in Southern California, but Dennie, not so much," she says. "He had to go on a union list to get a bricklaying job there and refused to consider anything else. Being so far from Iowa, he was pretty isolated from his family and friends. We were not getting along that well, as he didn't want me to do anything but stay home outside of my basketball obligations — which was pretty consistent with how it was in Iowa. I was in my early 20s and wanted to have fun and hated saying 'no' to all invitations, as Dennie was not interesting in doing much."

The tensions were indications of things to come.

L.A. to San Francisco

As for the season itself, it didn't last long, but it was still an adventure.

"One wild trip to Albuquerque, the team drove in two cars, with Ken Cole driving in front and I was in the back car, and we were supposed to keep up with him," Molly recalls. "We left in the early evening to drive all night (to save hotel money maybe), and he was seriously driving 90 miles an hour almost the whole way, which was over 12 hours, only stopping for gas. Of course, we didn't have phones or anything, so we were just trying to keep up, and I was riding in an older car with my teammate driver quite nervous about going that fast, but she was afraid of losing him."

Things were just as chaotic once the Breeze reached their destination.

"At the game in Albuquerque, Ken got really upset at the end. We were down by two, and I was clobbered on a shot, fell to the ground — and the ref called a 3-second lane violation, and we lost. He literally ran onto the court and tackled the ref and started choking him, and it took several people to pull him off. I was like, 'Wow, what did I get myself into?'"

Whatever it was, it didn't last long. Oakland and San Jose never even played a game, leaving the LPBA with just three teams.

On the court, the Breeze started off strong, and Molly picked up where she'd left off in the WBL, scoring 45 and 47 points in a pair of December wins over Phoenix. But the first game drew some biting criticism for the LPBA from the Flames' hometown newspaper, the *Arizona Republic*, in the second paragraph of its story on the opener: "The Ladies Professional Basketball Association is not a major league."

According to the story, the official scorer was a no-show, and two nuns from a neighboring high school wound up working the scoreboard and the clock. The male cheerleaders didn't know any of the cheers. The public-address announcer had never seen a pro basketball game. And members of the Mesa Community College women's team got in free because they owned the shot clock.

The owner had said he needed to average 3,000 fans in order to make a profit, but only half that showed up for the opener — when interest should have been at its highest. But that crowd was large compared to the number of fans who showed up to the second game against the Flames, on the Breeze's home court at Chapman College in Orange.

Paid attendance for that game was just 250 — despite an article advancing the Dec. 16 contest in the *Los Angeles Times*: about the same number that had showed up to watch the Cornets in Cedar Falls during a blizzard.

The size of the crowd didn't affect Molly's shooting, though, as she continued to pour in the points. Two days later against New Mexico, she scored 40, including a pair of 20-foot jumpers to stall a third-quarter rally by the Energee, a team led by former University of New Mexico coach Norm Ellenberger. The game ultimately turned into a 121-92 romp, and *The Times* headlined the story: "What's New? Bolin Scores 40."

But before Christmas, the Phoenix franchise called it quits, and the Breeze followed Dec. 30, leaving the Energee with no one to play. Ellenberger wouldn't give up that easily, though, as he began a campaign to get the team into the WBL. Molly, meanwhile, went back to Iowa for the holidays and soon was getting calls from WBL teams trying to recruit her. Mercurio had paid her what she was due from the Breeze, and she was ready to look at other options for her future.

"Looking back, I have no regrets about trying the LPBA, as it was the best choice presented at the time," she says. "None of the teams working the hardest to keep me in the WBL played in Year 3: Iowa, New York and Bill Byrne's attempt to put a WBL team in Tampa Bay. The league must have granted him a franchise for stepping down as commissioner, but he didn't get financial backing in time."

Steve Kirk, now coaching Nebraska, contacted Molly about joining the Wranglers, who had won five of their first six games before the New Year and led the Central Division.

"I knew they had a great team but wasn't that thrilled about going to Omaha," Molly says. "I wanted a new adventure!"

Seven of the league's nine teams contacted her to express interest, including the Dallas Diamonds, who already had Nancy Lieberman on their roster. Signing Molly would have given them perhaps the best backcourt in the history of women's pro basketball.

"I remember literally being on the phone nonstop for a few days, fielding calls from different teams," Molly says. "I remember taking notes and writing pros and cons, and I began to form a wish list of what I wanted in a contract."

Dallas assistant coach Tom Davis recalls that the Diamonds were "right there in the running" for Molly.

"A good reason for this was (Dallas owner) Michael Staver had always wanted her on his team — for dual purposes. Her marketability was phenomenal, so Dallas was prepared to offer her $20,000."

Davis says all signs pointed toward Dallas signing Molly until two things happened. "I'm not sure which was the more influential of the two actions," he says. "First, the (San Francisco) Pioneers fired Coach Frank LaPorte and hired ex-New York Stars coach Dean Meminger. Molly had always been an admirer of Dean's and wanted to play under him." Secondly, he continues, team president Dave Almstead expressed reservations about the need to sign a second superstar when the team already had Lieberman. "So here was the first bona-fide superstar that we could have gotten, because we had shown the most interest," Davis says. But it never happened.

Instead, Molly chose Meminger and the Pioneers, which allowed her to stay on the West Coast and reunite with former Cornets teammate Doris Draving, who had been waiting to play basketball since signing with a Tucson Storm team that had folded after a single game.

The Pioneers, unlike the Nebraska Wranglers, were struggling on the court. But they were coached by Meminger, who had coached the New York Stars to the previous year's title — only to find himself out of a job when the franchise folded. He hooked on with the Pioneers, who were looking to improve on the previous season's .500 record.

"The San Francisco Pioneers were in reorganization mode and were moving their players around to improve the team that got off to a slow start," Molly says. "They flew me to San Fran for a couple of days, and I was very impressed. They seemed financially stable, had just hired Dean Meminger to coach, had just signed my buddy and teammate Doris Draving, and were open to signing more Cornets. On top of all that, they were acceptable to everything on my wish list and put it into a contract. Given all those factors together, it was pretty much a no-brainer to move to San Francisco."

Meminger offered a contrast with Molly's previous coach, Steve Kirk. He wanted his players to be more creative on the court and criticized Kirk for, as Molly recalls, making his players "into robots."

Meminger himself was anything but robotic.

"Dean was quite the personality — he always dressed really sharp at games, and in practice wanted to play against us, or make us keep up with him when we were running," Molly says. "One time, he lined us all up to each take a charge from him because he wanted to toughen us up.

"He wasn't really easy to play for, but I always liked Dean, and he understood the game better than any other coach I had. He didn't even care what we did in our free time as long as we performed on the court. He pushed and challenged me in ways that helped me improve, and since that was the last WBL season, I never really got the chance to put that learning to good use — except when I was demonstrating at basketball camps."

Specifically, Meminger helped her to improve her "body mechanics" and her long-range jump shot. He urged her to use the power in her legs rather than relying on her upper body to maintain a proper shooting form, even from outside. In doing so, she was able to utilize the strength she had developed back at Moravia High when she was competing in the high jump and hurdles, rather than trying to outmuscle bigger players under the basket. That 30-inch vertical leap made up for a lot when it came to shooting over opponents and jumping to grab a loose ball.

Meminger also wanted Molly to become more efficient with her shooting: He wanted her to score the same number of points while taking fewer shots. He was a consummate strategist — so much so that he always seemed eager to talk basketball, even away from the court.

"He would often pull me aside for long periods of time to philosophize about the game and use me for a sounding board of what he was thinking about for the team," Molly says. "I didn't mind so much, except for the times after a game, when he would call me out of my hotel room and I would stand in the hallway to listen to him go on and on when I was half asleep standing up."

Meminger wanted to use a similar approach in San Francisco that had been successful for him in New York: Create a team that was two deep at each position, so 10 players could be rotated in and out seamlessly. He'd used that depth to wear down Iowa in the previous year's finals, but it never quite came together with the Pioneers, even though they had plenty of talent and the players bonded, on and off the court.

Molly, Joan Uhl, Doris Draving, Tanya Crevier and Sister Green were all former Cornets.

"The difference between the Cornets and the Pioneers was that the Cornets were more of a family, as we spent much more time together on the bus, in hotels, etc.," Draving recalls. "It was all so new and exciting to think that we were getting paid to do something we loved so much. We all just blended together so well.

"The Pioneers were more like being adopted by another family. Eventually, half of the original Cornets ended up in San Francisco with the Pioneers, and we began to jell and feel like a family again."

Other key players included Cindy Haugejorde, who also had ties to the Hawkeye State. The 6-foot-1 front-line player had scored more than 2,000 points for the University of Iowa and played more minutes than anyone else for the Pioneers in 1980-81. She ranked second on the team in both scoring average at 16.6 (behind Molly) and rebounds per game with 8.0 (behind Draving).

Then there was Cardte Hicks from Cal State-Northridge, the team's third-leading scorer at 14.7 points a game, who unleashed 41 in a late-season loss to the New Jersey Gems. Hicks, the first woman to dunk a basketball in competition, would join Molly and Haugejorde in the All-Star Game.

"My teammates on the Pioneers eventually became family like the Cornets — I was so lucky to have that happen again with a team, especially given the rocky road to get to that point," Molly says. "Roberta Williams, Musiette McKinney, Cindy, Cardte, Doris, Joan and Tanya were great to be around. Cindy and Doris in particular really made me laugh with their sense of humor. A group of teammates, including all the former Cornets and I, had two condos close to each other in Novato. So, we all piled into one car to go to practice across the Golden Gate Bridge every day. It was about an hour drive, so we did a lot of goofy stuff to entertain ourselves on the drive."

Molly played her first game with the Pioneers on Jan. 6, hitting 4 of 12 shots from the field and 5 of 5 free throws for 13 points in a 92-87 win over the hapless New England Gulls. San Francisco had already played seven games at that point, losing six of them, without her. With her, the Pioneers improved, going 5-6 in the remainder of their games before the All-Star Game.

One of those wins was a 104-102 overtime win over New England at Merrimack College, which was so far north of Boston that it was nearly on the New Hampshire state line. No wonder only 650 fans showed up.

But that was a big crowd compared with the 150 or so who turned out for the Gulls' scheduled game against the Pioneers four days later in Portland, Maine. You could hardly blame them: With snow in the forecast and low temperatures dipping below zero, it was hardly the kind of weather conducive to a night on the town.

The 7,000-seat Cumberland County Civic Center was like a graveyard when the Gulls walked into the arena. They said they hadn't been paid in a week and were living on "one meal a day," but the owner had promised to pay them from an expected $15,000 in ticket sales. When they saw the size of the crowd, the players knew there was no way the team would reach that figure.

So, they voted to strike and left the arena. Althea Gwyn, who had played for the New York Stars the previous year, was among the players who voted to walk away. When members of the Minnesota Fillies took similar action later in the season, Gwyn endorsed the move:

"They not only did the right thing, they got the idea from

us," she said.

Shortly after the Gulls left the building, the Pioneers arrived.

"We were on the East Coast in freezing weather to play the New England Gulls," Molly remembers. "We were given a locker room and put on our uniforms and went out to the floor to warm up. Unfortunately, this was the night the Gulls team chose to make a stance and not play unless they were paid."

The Pioneers soon found themselves as cash-poor as the Gulls, but for a different reason.

"When the word came down to the court that we were not going to get to play a game that night, Dean being Dean, decided to run a full practice since we were already dressed and on the court — so we worked out for about 90 minutes or so. When we went back to our locker room, all our things had been ransacked, despite security assurances that the door had been locked. There had been a high school team in our locker room that played a doubleheader in the gym earlier, before our game was scheduled, so we naturally thought they were the ones that went through our bags since they had come in the locker room after we left.

"Needless to say, we *all* lost all our meal cash — which was at least a couple hundred dollars each, since we had just started the road trip — plus I had my wedding ring, my high school class ring and another small diamond ring all stolen, never to be replaced. No insurance offered — nothing. I think our next game was in Minnesota, and Dean had to charge our meals on his card until some money was sent to cover us for food for the rest of the way. With 10 or 12 players, it had to have been a major heist."

The Pioneers lived to fight another day, but the Gulls weren't so fortunate. The team didn't play any more games after that, and the league officially revoked the franchise less than two weeks later, saying the team was in default to the league on "five or six points." The players immediately became free agents, with Gwyn and Chris Critelli landing with the Chicago Hustle, while Sister Green rejoined several of her former Iowa teammates in San Francisco.

Gwyn's rationale for choosing Chicago?

"They've never missed a paycheck."

All-Star again

The third-year All-Star Game was played in Albuquerque, which wasn't a WBL city at the time but had hosted a team in the recently defunct LPBA: the New Mexico Energee.

"Stormin' Norman" Ellenberger was lobbying to place an expansion team in Albuquerque the following season (which ultimately wasn't played), and had persuaded the league to schedule its third All-Star Game in the Land of Enchantment. Greg Williams, the former Houston assistant, had moved over to become head coach of the Dallas Diamonds after the Angels folded, and been chosen to coach in the All-Star Game. He recalls that Ellenberger insisted that Molly play in the game, even though she hadn't started the season with the league.

Molly had played in Albuquerque before with the Breeze, and Ellenberger knew he could market her to bring in the fans and fill the arena. She was placed on the West squad which already featured Nancy Lieberman and Carol Blazejowski. Sure enough, the sports headlines for the next two days featured photos of Molly with the news of the WBL All-Stars in town for the big game.

"He demanded that Molly be allowed to play in the All-Star Game," Williams says of Ellenberger. "Fortunately, she got put on the team I was coaching."

Molly wasn't in the starting lineup but hit 13 of 20 shots from the floor and all three of her free throws to leading the scoring with 29 points. Blazejowski and Lieberman added 20 each, but it was Molly the crowd wanted to see shoot, and she didn't disappoint them. In the third quarter, she hit seven consecutive shots, mostly from the top of the key, as the West opened up a 89-51 lead en route to a 125-92 blowout.

Molly with fellow San Francisco Pioneers all-stars Cindy Haugejorde, left, and Cardte Hicks.

"I loved it," Molly said of the crowd's cheering. "I've been here before, and I guess I had a following."

"What a performance!" Williams says. "She'd been playing in the other league and hadn't been playing any of the players in this league (very long). It was a whole lot more fun having Molly on your team than staring down the bench and seeing her in an Iowa Cornets uniform."

After the game, Meminger took back what he'd said about asking Molly not to take so many shots.

Molly recalls: "Afterward, Dean pulled me aside and said he owed me an apology, and I said, 'For what?' He said he realized he was wrong about me after watching the All-Star Game and to forget what he said about taking fewer shots per game. He said, 'From now on — you have the green light to play your game your way.' So, the rest of the season things were a lot less restricted, and a lot more fun!"

In all, it was a great experience. Molly is one of only four WBL players — along with Althea Gwyn, Paula Mayo and Janice Thomas — to earn All-Star and All-Pro honors all three seasons.

"I was happy that I had established among my peers that I deserved to be there" at the All-Star Game, Molly says. "It was such a great night to experience, but the phone call and grim news from (Steve) Kirk early the following morning brought all those feelings crashing down."

The call from her former coach didn't have anything to do with basketball. He was calling with news that Connie Kunzmann, Molly's former teammate in Iowa, was missing.

Kirk himself was in Albuquerque for the All-Star Game when he got word about Kunzmann, who had joined his Nebraska Wranglers after the Cornets folded. She had been at the heart of the Iowa teams that made two consecutive finals, averaging more than eight points and nearly seven rebounds a game during the Cornets' first season, then improving on those numbers in Year 2, when she pulled down more than eight rebounds while averaging nearly 10 points. She also ranked fifth in the league in steals, once producing 11 in a single game, and had scored 20 points in the Game 4 loss to the New York Stars in the 1980 championship series. But she'd been forced to find a new team when the Cornets folded during the offseason.

Molly had tried to persuade her to go west with her, but Kunzmann wanted to stay close to home.

"When the Cornets were unable to find a new owner for Season 3, I began talking to Connie about going with me and trying the new league in California," Molly says. "However, Steve Kirk, who had taken the coaching job for the Nebraska

Wranglers, was the more aggressive recruiter because he knew the value Connie brought to any team's front court. But the deciding factor was that Omaha was close to her hometown of Everly, Iowa: less than a three-hour drive."

It was also just a short drive from Wayne State College, her alma mater, where she had all but rewritten the record book.

Kunzmann wasn't a starter in Omaha, but she was named captain of the Wranglers, who were on their way to winning the league title. She appeared to be coming into her own Feb. 5 when the Wranglers went on the road to face Nancy Lieberman and the Dallas Diamonds in a clash between division leaders. Dallas won the game, but Kunzmann scored 19 points on 8 of 9 shooting and grabbed 10 rebounds in what Lieberman called "the game of her life."

The following night, with the Wranglers back in Omaha, Kunzmann was in a mood to relax. Coach Kirk was bound for Albuquerque to coach in the All-Star Game, and the team had a few days off, so she threw on her old Cornets jacket and headed for a bar called Tiger Tom's on the northwest side of town.

She stayed there until closing, when she accepted a ride from a security guard named Lance Tibke, whom she'd met once previously, and he drove her to a cemetery.

That was the last time anyone saw her alive.

The next time anyone saw Tibke, he had a black eye and, on Feb. 10 — the day after the All-Star Game — he confessed to her murder: They had gotten into a fight at the cemetery, and he had beaten her over the head with a tire iron, burying her bloody Cornets jacket nearby and dumping her body in the Missouri River. The jacket was found a week later; her body wasn't recovered until March, when the harsh winter weather finally broke, and a search party found it tangled in the limbs of a tree that had fallen into water.

"We were all devastated when her life was tragically cut short, but the memories of the good times will always stay with me and the rest of her teammates," Molly says. "She lived her life with a zest and enthusiasm that will never be forgotten, and I was fortunate to be her friend."

Molly vs. Nancy

Molly and Lieberman had played together at the All-Star Game, but they had yet to meet as opponents on the court. When they did, it was in one of the WBL's most bizarre games.

Once again, Williams had a role to play, as did his assistant, Tom Davis.

As they had for Molly's matchup against Liz Silcott in St. Louis the previous season, the media turned up the hype machine for the Feb. 27 game in San Francisco, billing it as something akin to a heavyweight title bout between Molly and Nancy. Davis recalls that the San Francisco newspapers ran a big spread on Molly leading up to the game, and the marquee out front of the Civic Auditorium where the game was to be played, billed the game as "San Francisco Pioneers vs. Nancy Lieberman and the Dallas Diamonds."

On the day of the game, the arena was filled with fans eager to welcome their team back after a four-game road trip and hoping to see the Pioneers snap a six-game losing streak. Dallas had won all four of the games between the two teams that season, and this would be the Pioneers' last chance for revenge.

"The place was packed," Williams recalls "They had maybe 3,000 people there, and the atmosphere was electric."

The crowd was so loud, according to Davis, that it sounded like three or four times that many people were there.

One of the most important people in the arena, however,

wasn't in the crowd or even wearing a team uniform. He was an official that Williams describes as looking "like he spent an hour in the locker room before the game poofing his pompadour."

Davis recalls nicknaming the guy Gorgeous George, "because during the games, he would always caress his hair, making sure it was in place."

"Gorgeous George" almost immediately began focusing on Lieberman, who seemingly couldn't make a move on offense without a whistle blowing. She picked up her third personal foul barely halfway through the first quarter and had to leave the game to avoid picking up a fourth. When she wasn't getting whistled for fouls, she was being called for traveling: She finished the game with 16 turnovers. Williams remembers: "Literally every time Nancy touched the ball and made a move, this guy would come over and do the fist-over-fist traveling call," Williams says. "She was so frustrated."

Williams became frustrated, too, and got whistled for a technical in the opening period for arguing the charge that gave Lieberman her third foul. But even though Lieberman was watching from the bench, the Diamonds went on a 12-1 run to take a seemingly commanding 39-21 lead 3½ minutes into the second quarter.

Williams vowed never to get a second technical in a game, because he didn't want to be ejected, but something happened in the third quarter that pushed him beyond his limit.

"In the second half, Molly is driving the baseline and she kind of gets under the basket; we foul her, and Molly passes the ball. This hot-dog official comes up and yells, 'Two shots!' He said, 'She was going to shoot until you fouled her.' I just went crazy, and he T'd me up."

The crowd got even louder, breaking into chants of "Na-na!

na-na-*na*-na! Na-na-*na*-na! Hey hey-ey! Goodbye!" as the ref ejected Williams from the game. Williams, however, refused to leave, thinking he could stay and simply accept a $10,000 fine. (Davis' take: "A good choice, because no one every pays their fines in the WBL anyway!") A security guard was finally called to escort him from the bench him off the court to the tunnel, where he was able to see just a small part of the court. Davis was left to assume the coaching duties.

Davis says he was hoping Williams would at least pause to give him some advice before leaving.

No such luck.

"I thought, 'Just please come back and say something.' But now I am on my own with 10 wide-eyed players, who can't believe what they have just seen. Greg makes a slow exit past the Pioneers bench as he adjusts his coat and points a threatening finger at the refs. Greg has now left the arena."

Dallas continued to hold the advantage, though, building a 77-70 lead before the Pioneers bounced back with a 16-8 run to take their first lead of the game at 86-85 early in the fourth period. Molly hit a pair of free throws with 9½ minutes left to give San Francisco a 92-87 lead, but then it was the Diamonds' turn to respond, scoring 12 unanswered points.

It was a see-saw affair the rest of the way. At one point, Molly hit a 17-foot jumper to pull the Pioneers within a point at 106-105, but Lieberman responded with a turnaround 16-footer at the other end. The Pioneers' Cardte Hicks, scored four of her 34 points on back-to-back baskets that put the Pioneers on top again at 111-110.

The Pioneers led 115-112 when Lieberman was fouled with 2 seconds left; Williams remembers hoping Davis would tell Lieberman: If you make the first shot, miss the second on purpose, so we can try to get the offensive rebound. Davis shouted out to Lieberman to do just that: "I'm quite sure she was already thinking along those lines, but for my ego, I'll say I told her."

From his place in the tunnel, Williams couldn't see the foul line, but he could see the scoreboard, which changed by one point when the first foul shot was made. He heard the crowd react when the second shot was missed, and then a collective groan. He waited to see whether the score would change again: It did. The Diamonds had gotten the rebound and scored, forcing overtime.

By that time, Lieberman had fouled out, part of a whistle-fest marred by 76 personal foul calls that featured 116 free-throw attempts. There were so many interruptions, the game took three hours to play.

"I'm lucky my teammates left me comp tickets, or I couldn't have seen this game," Lieberman quipped afterward.

Even without Lieberman, the Diamonds managed to prevail in overtime, 129-128. And despite the refs' interference, the Molly-versus-Nancy show had lived up to its billing. Molly finished with a game-high 35 points, while Lieberman scored 33 to lead the Diamonds.

Molly guards Dallas' Nancy Lieberman, an exciting matchup in two leagues – the WBL and the WABA.

On the road again

The loss dropped San Francisco to 6-17 on the season as the Pioneers went back on the road for a five-game stretch, during which they won just once. That brutal portion of their schedule — 10 road games in 11 days, with their only home game against Dallas — ended any playoff homes they might have had.

There was a reason for the extended road trips:

"They strung all the road games together to save money on travel," Molly says. "This meant I was on the road for a lot longer periods of time than what we were used to." In mid-February, there was a six-day gap between a game in Dallas and one in New Orleans, 500 miles to the east.

"After the Dallas game, the team flew into New Orleans to stay for almost a week before our game, rather than fly back to San Francisco," Molly explains. "Lucky for us, all the Mardi Gras parades and parties had started and, of course, we enjoyed the hell out of it. Once Dean (Meminger) was onto us and realized a couple of girls were hung over, so we ran for almost the whole practice. It was hot and humid, with no air conditioning in the gym, so several girls got sick — but I don't remember being one of them. I've never been a big drinker, because I *will* definitely get sick."

Whether it was the hangovers, the long layoff or something else, the Pioneers fell to the New Orleans Pride, 126-113.

Another money-saving quirk in the schedule called for San Francisco to play back-to-back games in New Jersey against the Gems and the league's other major star, Carol Blazejowski.

Like Molly, Blazejowski was a scorer. She had averaged 34 points a game during her junior year at Montclair State, and had topped that during her senior season, when she averaged 38.6. She had been the leading scorer on the national team that won the 1979 World Championships in South Korea and was poised to represent her country in the 1980 Olympics before the U.S. boycott derailed those plans. So she had switched gears, signing a three-year, $150,000 contract with the New Jersey Gems that made her the league's highest-paid player.

In their first meeting, just a few days after Molly rejoined the WBL, Blazejowski had scored 36 points as the Gems won at home 119-104. But two months later, it was a different story. Blazejowski still got her points (34 of them) but Molly topped that total with 38. Still, the Pioneers lost again, 129-113, before a record crowd of 2,617 at South Mountain Arena in West Orange, N.J. The big difference: New Jersey hit 46 of 61 free throws compared to just 21 of 29 for San Francisco.

The second of the two back-to-back games was another disappointment for the Pioneers, who fell 115-106 despite 41 points from Cardte Hicks and 22 from Molly. This left the Pioneers with just two more games on their schedule against the Gems, who had won each of their first five meetings. It was scheduled for March 25, 1981 at San Francisco Civic Auditorium and came on the heels of a 104-98 upset of Nebraska two days earlier.

Molly, who led the way with 28 points against the Wranglers, hit a short jumper with 24 seconds left to put the Pioneers ahead for good in that one, but it was just a warmup for her final game of the season against Blazejowski and the Gems.

She finished with 40 points to Blazejowski's 31, but, as *The San Francisco Examiner* put it: "The irony was that Moly Bolin's best move of the night came when she didn't have the ball." That move occurred with less than 2 minutes left and the Pioneers leading 121-117, the Gems having shaved nine points off San Francisco's lead entering the fourth quarter.

Molly, who had grown up playing offense almost

exclusively in Iowa's 6-on-6 game, showed she wasn't just a scorer. Even in her high school days, she had looked for an opportunity to play defense after a missed free throw forced the other team's backcourt players to bring the ball up the floor: "When they had someone who had some ballhandling issues," she recalls, "I would try to steal the ball when they were bringing it up the court."

Flash forward again to the game against the Pioneers. The Gems' Janice Thomas had the ball, with a chance to cut the lead to two, when Molly ran up from behind her and knocked the ball away and off Thomas out of bounds.

Pioneers' ball.

"I saw she had her back turned," Molly said at the time. "She didn't know I was there. It was a crucial time, because if they got down and scored again, the lead would have been down to two. So, I tried to mess things up."

After a foul on the inbounds, San Francisco's Musiette McKinney made a pair of free throws.

"From then on, everything was OK," Molly said.

The free throws began a 6-0 closing run that gave San Francisco a 128-117 win.

The Pioneers had each of their last eight games at home and, although they were out of playoff contention, they prevailed in seven of them (including a forfeit win over St. Louis) — the only defeat being a two-point loss in their final game against New Jersey. They closed the year in decisive fashion, building a 90-38 lead after three quarters in annihilating the Minnesota Fillies 122-61.

There was a reason it was so one-sided: These weren't the real Fillies. The actual team had walked out a couple of weeks earlier because they hadn't been paid, and the franchise had filled their roster spots with what amounted to a pickup team.

Molly scored 27 points in a balanced attack, cementing her season average at 26.7 points a game, second only to Blazejowski. The Pioneers still finished last in their division, and the Nebraska team they'd beaten eight days before the end of the season wound up winning the title, slipping past Dallas in a five-game series.

Molly's 40-point games			
Date	**Opponent**	**Score**	**Points**
	Iowa vs.		
Jan. 28, 1979	Milwaukee	116-105	40*
March 27, 1979	Minnesota	126-109	53*
Nov. 27, 1979	Chicago	122-111	44
Dec. 16, 1979	New Jersey	100-108 (L)	42
Dec. 27, 1979	St. Louis	106-115 (L)	42
Jan. 13, 1980	Minnesota	109-103	54*
Feb. 7, 1980	St. Louis	107-97	47
Feb. 21, 1980	New York	131-125	41
March 2, 1980	Minnesota	125-85	55*
March 9, 1980	St. Louis	101-81	40
March 29, 1980	Minnesota (playoffs)	128-111	50**
April 8, 1980	New York (finals)	119-112	49
	S. California (LPBA) vs.		
Nov. 29, 1980	Tucson	118-78	41
Dec. 12, 1980	Phoenix	93-87	45
Dec. 16, 1980	Phoenix	98-83	47
Dec. 18, 1980	New Mexico	121-92	40
	San Francisco vs.		
Feb. 11, 1981	Chicago	143-116	41***
March 5, 1981	Minnesota	112-108	40
March 25, 1981	New Jersey	128-117	40

*Single-game record
**Playoff record
***Tied team record

It was still quite a turnaround for the Diamonds, who had finished last in their division the previous year with a woeful 7-28 record. With Lieberman on their roster, they did a complete 180 and finished at 27-9, tied with Nebraska for the league's best record. Off the court, however, it was a different story as the team struggled to meet its payroll.

"My lunch became a Diet Coke and a packet of peanut butter crackers," Williams says. "I was literally broke. I was riding my bike to work and eating that (kind of lunch) because it was all I could afford."

When the team owner noticed that Williams was looking for part-time jobs to supplement his income, he told the coach he was calling a 3 p.m. meeting for that afternoon. It was there that he announced the team was going out of business. Williams, who was owed a good deal of back pay, received a $30,000 settlement, but wasn't able to collect any of it.

Not only did the Diamonds fold, the WBL itself was soon history.

"What killed the WBL was that owners could not keep up financially," Doris Draving says. "Mr. Nissen always made sure the Cornets were paid, but not many teams could say that. Also, I do not think the world was ready for or interested in watching women play ball. We were way ahead of our time."

A pro without a league

At first, Molly held out hope that the WBL would live to fight another day. The condo lease expired, so her husband took their son Damien back to Iowa, but Molly stayed in San Francisco for a couple of weeks before following. The family was able to stay at her parents' house, because they were away while her father was working a job out of town.

"The word coming in was that the future of the league looked bleak," she says. "But I had dealt with three years of the league being described as 'fledgling' and didn't dwell on it while doing everything I possibly could to help it succeed and always hoping for the best."

Her husband, who had been promised jobs in California as part of her agreement to move West, had watched as they failed to materialize and "was pretty much done moving somewhere else because of basketball," Molly says, "and I did not blame him for feeling this way." He was looking forward to staying in Moravia and reconnecting with his contacts there so he could go back to work.

"But for me, I wasn't even close to being done with what I had started and worked for over the years. After experiencing the success I had in women's pro basketball, it was impossible for me to move back to Moravia without feeling like a total failure. I tried to envision a future of what I would do if I just stayed there, and it felt like a dark cloud of depression. Plus, if I tried to do the 'right thing' for my family and give it a try to live there for a year or two — what if I got stuck and had no opportunities to go anywhere else after the fame of the league died down?

"I just. Couldn't. Do it. Even though I knew it was selfish, I was 23 years old and wanted to live my life. When I was offered a chance to go to California and stay with a teammate at her parents' house until I could find a job ... I jumped at it, left Iowa and told Damien it would only take a few weeks to get settled and I would be back for him."

Molly's parents weren't happy with her decision. A friend's son had moved out to California, never to be heard from again, and they were convinced that the West Coast was like a black hole that swallowed people up. As it turned out, Molly did move out to California and has lived there ever since, but she didn't disappear off the face of the earth and would return to Moravia several times over the years.

Molly and Dennie agreed to divorce and share custody of Damien, and she flew out to California, where former teammate Joan Uhl had started a job working for a construction firm that was renovating Victorian homes. Molly got a job there, too, and started working on an old home that the company had purchased for $1 with the intent of moving it to a new site and completely remodeling it.

Her first task: to scrape all the mortar off a pile of old bricks from fireplaces in the home so they could be reused in the project.

"I admit it was really discouraging when I showed up for work that first day in my tank top and shorts, and seeing what my job was going to be for the next couple of weeks," she says. "It was boring, tedious work that never seemed to end, but when I found out there were bets going on that I couldn't handle this job and would quit — that was the last thing I was going to do."

The job after that wasn't any better. It involved scraping off rubber-backed carpet that had been glued onto an apartment's hardwood floor. After that, she was assigned to work "shoveling up, bagging and cleaning a huge pile of trash that tenants had thrown into a garage instead of the Dumpster." The work, she says, was "really disgusting, especially as we got down to the bottom of the pile and came across several wriggling, living creatures."

"At that point, the boss figured if I was going to stick around, they'd better train me to do more skilled work. So, I learned to paint and roof houses, starting with a two-story with the pitch so steep we had to be tied off at the peak to prevent falling off."

Molly had a new home and a steady income, but she was — for the time being, anyway — out of sports. And a new challenge lay ahead that had nothing to do with the court ... at least, not with a basketball court.

Custody battle

"After the third WBL season, I went back to Iowa for the summer. Things had been difficult for the last couple of years, and Dennie wanted to stay in Iowa and go back to work.

"I did not want to stay, so we agreed to divorce and share joint custody of Damien. I was a completely different person after all the experiences I had with the league than I was when I got married at age 18.

"But it was a friendly separation, and I sent Dennie and his friends on a trip to Las Vegas and California that included a stop at our storage to pick up his things and bring back in a trailer. We were getting along pretty well and agreed to share Damien, so I had no idea what was to come.

"I found out our divorce was not finalized six months later, when Dennie planned to get remarried and needed me to sign papers. We still had joint custody of Damien, but I insisted on having him go to school with me. However, I made a mistake of signing divorce papers that didn't specify physical custody."

The divorce was finally official in February of 1982.

"In the summer of 1982, I got a call in middle of night from a sheriff from Iowa (who said) that Dennie planned to take Damien from his school without my knowledge," Molly says.

The officer later said he found out about that plan from his ex-wife — who had remarried Dennie Bolin's brother. As a *Des Moines Register* columnist pointed out in the Dec. 5, 1982 edition, "justice often gets tangled in these small communities."

That phone tip from the officer was just the beginning.

When Molly heard about the plan, she says, "I pulled Damien from school, then later invited Dennie and his new wife to my house to work out and sign a new agreement regarding physical custody arrangements — Damien could go back to Iowa for a few weeks to visit but would come back in time to start school in California.

"Dennie enrolled Damien in kindergarten in Moravia but assured me it was just temporary because he 'wanted to go' and no problem — just come back as agreed, and I could pick him up after school."

But when Molly arrived at school to pick him up, Damien was nowhere to be seen: She watched all the kids file out, with no sign of him, and later found out he wasn't in that day at all. In fact, she later discovered, he had been taken to stay in a location far from Moravia, and Dennie had filed for full custody and an injunction to prevent Damien from leaving Iowa.

It took Molly a week to get a court date, but she spent $1,000 in filing fees and attorney costs to challenge the injunction. She'd spend more than that before all was said and done.

"Then I presented the signed agreement, from the day in my apartment, regarding physical custody to the judge, all the time thinking I could get things cleared up and go home with him right away."

It didn't work out that way. Instead, after a daylong hearing, the judge came back into the courtroom and announced he wouldn't be able to rule on this case because of his relationship to Dennie's attorney, leaving the injunction in place until she could get a hearing before a different judge.

Another case of that tangled justice. Or, as Molly observes: "The curse of small towns (is that) almost everyone is related somehow."

Molly returned to California. It wasn't until several weeks later that she got word a new hearing had finally been scheduled at the Appanoose County courthouse in Centerville, about 12 miles south of Moravia.

Molly and Damien

"I went through two full days of the opposing lawyer parading witness after witness answering questions that were either irrelevant to the case or not accurate," she says.

The *San Francisco Chronicle* story — which featured the Breeze publicity photo of her in a swimsuit — was introduced to insinuate she was somehow an unfit mother. The opposing counsel said the story was brought up "not for the picture," but because it contained information about her basketball career supposedly hindering her ability to be a good parent. Nonetheless, the picture was part of the package, and as any good journalist will tell you, a picture captures the reader's attention long before the contents of a story.

"I sat there incredulous as I realized their main line of attack was my basketball career," Molly recalls. "They referred to many stories from the newspapers, with many misquotes, about how I admitted that basketball had made things difficult for my family with the travel and constant moving, but I continued to do it anyway."

Dennie's lawyer proceeded to go through Molly's basketball schedule game by game in an attempt to show she had left her family to play on the road. As he "droned on and on," Molly realized that he was running the equivalent of a four-corner offense in basketball, stalling for time and hoping to run out the clock. At the end of the day, he asked for an indefinite continuance to focus on other cases. The judge granted this request, forcing Molly to go back to California yet again and await word on when the hearing would resume.

While all this was going on, Molly received an offer to play professionally in Italy, but she had to turn it down because "there is no way I was leaving and then later I decided I couldn't go and take Damien with me because it wasn't in his best interest."

Dennie's lawyer had taken up so much time presenting his case during the first part of the hearing that Molly hadn't even had a chance to present her side of the story ... which she finally did when she returned to Iowa for a third time and the case started up again.

"I was confident that we had clearly won the case with clear-cut evidence that couldn't be denied. The judge said he would mail his ruling to us, but when I got it a couple of weeks later, it was word for word, verbatim of the final argument that Dennie's lawyer had presented."

The judge, Richard Vogel, awarded sole custody to Dennie, allowing Molly to have Damien for just two months during the summer and forcing her to pay $25 a week in child support. He wrote that "the turning point" in reaching a decision was the fact that Damien was enrolled in Moravia schools and had lived with Dennie for 11 of the previous 15 months; both sets of grandparents also lived in Moravia, he said.

This failed to take into account, however, that — as Molly's lawyer, Ione Shadduck, pointed out — "the reason the father had custody all that time was because he would not let the boy have access to his mother. Molly would have had Damien a lot of that time if she could have."

As the process played out in the courtroom, the town of Moravia split into factions about the case, with some residents supporting Molly and others backing Dennie.

Molly's parents were so shaken by the ugliness of the dispute that they put their home on the market, with plans to move to the Sun Belt.

"I can't face anybody," Wanda Van Benthuysen said. "It's not that I'm ashamed, but so many stories have been made up to make Molly look bad, I can't stand it anymore."

They didn't end up leaving, after all, but it took its toll. In a town of 700 people, a lot of people know about the small stuff, not to mention a case that grabs headlines in Des Moines and involves a nationally known athlete who all but put Moravia on the map.

Having lost at the hearing, Molly had two choices: She could accept the ruling, or she could appeal to the Iowa Supreme Court.

"I went through a short period of being devastated before I decided I couldn't and wouldn't accept that ruling," he says.

But her lawyer said an appeal would be expensive: It would cost $2,500 just to start the process. Molly didn't have the money, and she couldn't find anyone willing to lend it to her: "They said I had already lost in court, and it didn't make sense for me to go deeper into debt and lose again."

"I kept going back to Ione in desperation when I couldn't get the money, and she kept lowering the amount, and I *still* couldn't get the money. Finally, exasperated, she said, 'Look, we are running out of time to appeal. If you can get $500 to me right away, I will get it started. My parents then drove to Des Moines and paid her."

Once the case got to the Iowa Supreme Court, the momentum turned 180 degrees.

"It was a pretty timely process, and I think there were seven judges because I had to pay for each to get a full transcript of the case; thanks to Dennie's lawyer, it was about 3 inches thick!" Molly says. "But the ruling came down in July 1983 — almost a year from when this drama started — and it was a unanimous ruling in my favor."

Damien was 6 when the court issued its decision, which highlighted the crux of the issue: joint custody and physical custody were two different things under an Iowa statute passed just one year earlier. According to the law, joint custody did "not require physical care," stipulating that a judge could "award physical care to one parent only."

"We believe the problem between the parties was not the issue of joint custody but physical care," the court wrote, adding that the "failure to have an agreement on that issue at the time of the decree inevitably contributed to the subsequent problem."

But the court saved its real criticism for the judge in the case. The lower court had erred in granting Dennie sole custody, it said, on several grounds. Among them, it found that Molly had "gone 'the extra mile' to support Dennie's relationship with Damien," but that the other side had "tried to achieve a de facto victory in the dispute over physical care by alienating Damien from his mother."

"Molly's right as joint custodian, however, should not be defeated on this basis," the opinion continued. On the contrary, the panel ruled that Dennie "had simply not given joint custody a chance to work."

The Supreme Court reversed and remanded the lower court order, awarding Molly physical custody of Damien during the school year.

"Not very long after the Supreme Court ruling, I met with Dennie and told him that I forgave them all and knew they thought they were protecting Damien.

"I was so glad to put that behind me and move on. Shortly after this was when all the exciting things started to happen in basketball again."

Rick Barry gives Molly five after she beat him in a game of H-O-R-S-E.
Photo by Bob Modersohn

After the WBL

During her playing career, Molly shared the court with some famous names. Pete Maravich in *Dribble* was just the beginning. Then there was the time when Magic Johnson called her up to the podium when she was helping to kick off the LPBA and the Breeze.

Before she left to join the Breeze, she played a friendly

game of H-O-R-S-E against Rick Barry, the former Golden State Warriors star who had just retired. Barry, known for his incredibly accurate underhanded free throws, was (and is) the only player ever to lead the NCAA, ABA and NBA in scoring for a single season.

But he found himself up against more than he could handle in Molly.

Barry, 36 at the time, had gone to Des Moines to appear at an event to benefit Special Olympics at the Des Moines Center of Science and Industry. Molly, of course, had to duplicate Barry's patented underhanded foul shot, but he was unable to match her successful shot from halfcourt, which sealed the victory.

Although Molly didn't attempt many 3-point shots in the WBL, it wasn't because she couldn't hit from that distance. The game was different then: The 3-point shot was less an integral part of basketball and was used more as a Hail Mary if a team was down by three in the waning seconds.

In the first eight years after the NBA added the 3-point shot to its arsenal in 1979, the most any player ever hit in a single season was 92. Today, by contrast, players like Stephen Curry and James Harden launch 3-point shots at will: Curry set a record for them with 402 in the 2015-16 season.

And 2016 was the year an article appeared under headline: "Steph Curry ... The 'Male Machine Gun Molly'?"

Cat Ariail, a PhD history student at the University of Miami, wrote in that piece: "Bolin possessed a quick-release jumper that allowed her to shoot over often bigger defenders, a strategy that resembles that of Steph Curry (coincidentally, Bolin also sported a number 30 jersey). She also scored many of these buckets by pulling up after a single quick-dribble move."

Molly hasn't taken the court with Curry, but she did do a

commercial with Larry Bird in 1984 to promote Spalding basketballs.

"Of course, I was thrilled for that opportunity, and it was an incredible experience," she says. "Thanks to Spalding, I got the full VIP treatment, with limo rides to and from the airport

Molly with Larry Bird during their Spalding basketball commercial shoot.

and the best of everything. On the day of the commercial shoot, I shot around, and played a little one-on-one with Larry Bird. I impressed him with my shooting, but one-on-one was *no* contest of course, so we mostly goofed around.

"I remember walking into a room where a makeup artist was getting us camera ready, and couldn't resist teasing him as they were applying his makeup. I said, 'Oh, so this is your usual pregame routine for your televised games?' He laughed and was a good sport that day, and I found him to be very nice and respectful but also kind of quiet and shy."

Bird and Barry weren't the only male players to shoot hoops with Molly; of course, she'd started playing against guys as a schoolgirl in Moravia, and once the WBL folded, she stayed in shooting shape by taking on the guys again.

"At first, I played against the guys to improve my game, then later on it was because it was the only opportunity available to me to play at all," Molly says.

She played in several men's recreational leagues — mostly

in Southern California, but also one in Iowa — although she stayed in the 6-feet-and-under category. ("I just wasn't the type of player to battle with bigger guys for rebounds.")

Occasionally, however, such opportunities did arise. In December of 1982, she entered a national 3-on-3 women's tournament sponsored by Foot Locker along with her former teammate Joan Uhl and Robbie Beyer, who had been a teammate of Uhl's at Cal Poly-Pomona. Reserve Chris O'Sullivan rounded out the squad. The team defeated Ann Meyers' defending championship team en route to the finals at the Forum in Inglewood, where they lost to a team from Cerritos on a last-second shot.

The event drew big crowds to the Forum, then the Lakers' home court, with nearly 15,000 fans turning out for the quarterfinals and a capacity crowd of 17,505 on hand for the semis.

Next up, in February of 1983, was a tour involving two women's all-star teams organized by Nancy Lieberman, who had been working with tennis star Martina Navratilova on strength training. Some of Navratilova's sponsors signed on to back the tour, which featured mostly former WBL players, and Molly was among a group that stayed overnight at Navratilova's house before it got started.

"She is one of the nicest, most genuine people I've ever met, not to mention generous," Molly says of the tennis great. "Some of her endorsements had expired, and multiple international companies had sent her boxes and boxes of clothing, shoes and socks in hopes of signing her. But Martina gave all of it away to us starving basketball players, and we had to mail boxes home to ourselves, we had so much stuff."

The tour featured several games in Texas before returning for its finale at the Forum, where Molly got a temporary job to promote the tour. She expected about 5,000 fans to turn out for that last game, but only about 1,000 made it, kept away by a bad storm and the series finale of *M*A*S*H*.

Despite the disappointing crowd, Molly's time at the Forum turned out to be a lot of fun.

"The year 1983 was a great time to be working at the Forum because the NBA All-Star Game was held there on Feb. 13," Molly says. "I was given tickets and sat low at midcourt with Roy Johnson, a writer from *Sports Illustrated* who did a story on me on 1981, and had an all access pass to the private clubs. I remember thinking, 'Wow! This is a long way from Moravia, Iowa!'

One afternoon, she was taking a break and went into the arena, where she sat about halfway down to watch the Lakers practice. They were, at the time, the reigning NBA champs, having defeated the Philadelphia 76ers in 1982 for their second title in three years. (They would win three more titles in the next six years, making the Finals five times.)

But one of the Lakers in the arena at the time was famous from an earlier era, when the team had battled the Celtics for supremacy during the 1960s.

"As I was intently watching some drills, somebody came and sat beside me and said, 'Well, what do you think?'" Molly recalls. "I looked over, and it was freaking Jerry West, who was at the time the Lakers' general manager, and a major idol of mine because of his incredible jump shot. I told him that it looked to me like another NBA championship team with the addition of rookie, James Worthy.

"We chatted for a while about the technical aspects of the game, and I told him how I was working there to promote women's pro basketball and hoped for another shot to play professionally again. Eventually, I couldn't help but completely nerd out and ask him if I could have an autographed photo. He found one from when he coached the Lakers and signed it for me!"

Also during her time at the Forum, Molly gave an interview to an *L.A. Times* reporter who wrote a story about her career and touched on her precedent-setting custody case. The article drew the attention of movie producers, and Molly started getting calls asking about the rights to her story. She signed a contract, but no film ever got made; the process would repeat itself after *NBC SportsWorld* did a segment on her the following year, again without any movie being produced.

In the spring of 1983 or '84, Molly played some high-level pickup games against current and former USC and UCLA women players: "Someone got access to a gym, and some of the best competitive basketball I've ever played, outside of my teams, was in this time period."

Then she had another go at the national 3-on-3 tourney with Uhl ("the key inside person on our 3-on-3 teams"), this time with Lieberman as a teammate. The trio won the women's division easily and also entered the men's 6-feet-and-under category, where they did well until they ran into top-level competition. Even then, they lost only by a point or two.

At least one player on one of the women's teams, however, didn't take too kindly to Lieberman's style of play. "Nancy played very physical, as she learned on the streets against guys, and wasn't above grabbing and holding a jersey anytime she deemed necessary," Molly says. "Once, after beating out a women's team in the semifinals, we were in the locker room to change our shirts. When Nancy had the shirt over her head, one of our recent opponents came up, punched her in the mouth and ran. It was a cheap shot and most likely born out of the frustration with the physical way Nancy had played her."

All-stars who played against the U.S. Olympic team in 1984. Front: Cindy Ely, Carol Blazejowski, Tara Heiss, Holly Warlick, Molly, Debbie Groover, Barbara Robinson. Back: Jody Conradt (assistant coach), Sue Gunter (head coach), Nancy Lieberman, Heidi Wayment, Nancy Dunkle, Gail Marquis, Barbara Gill (manager), Toby Toburen (trainer).

Olympic All-Stars

In May of 1978, the International Olympic Committee awarded the '84 Summer Olympics to Los Angeles. That was still six years down the road, and little did fans of women's basketball know that they'd have to wait the entire six years to see Team USA in action for a second time.

The first time, in 1976, the team had unexpectedly won a silver medal — behind prohibitive favorite Russia — and, with the likes of Carol Blazejowski and Nancy Lieberman planning to compete, Team USA had positioned itself as a favorite for the 1980 gold in Moscow.

The U.S. Olympic boycott derailed those hopes, but with the 1984 Games on American soil (and with the Russians engaging in a tit-for-tat boycott of their own), expectations were even higher. Blazejowski and Lieberman had gone pro, but there was an influx of new talent to replace them.

Among the players on the '84 squad were 6-foot-8 center Ann Donovan from Old Dominion, who had averaged 20 points and 14.5 rebounds in a game during her college career; and USC forwards Cheryl Miller and Pam McGee, who had led the Trojans to two straight national titles. Miller, who also happened to be the sister of future NBA Hall of Famer Reggie Miller, was even more impressive in her own right: A four-time All-American, she was the most valuable player in two consecutive national championship tournaments.

The team would go unbeaten in eight games and sweep to the gold medal with an 85-55 rout of South Korea in the finals, but first, it would have to go up against a team of pro all-stars led by Molly, Carol Blazejowski and Nancy Lieberman.

Molly had been selected, along with Cornets teammate Doris Draving, to be part of a similar pre-Olympic all-star squad in 1980, but that team had never been assembled because of the boycott. Now, she had another chance.

The 1984 All-Stars and Team USA played a series of exhibitions as part of doubleheaders headlined by a game between the men's Olympic team and a group of NBA players. One of the exhibitions was even in Iowa.

"That," Molly says, "was my Olympics. It was an incredible experience all around and the *only* Olympic experience I was ever going to get since I had played pro and was ineligible to try out for the Olympic team."

The experience began with several days around the Fourth of July weekend at the Olympic Training Center in Colorado, where the all-stars assembled to practice, followed by the exhibition tour. Then came the tour: One game, at the Hoosier Dome in Indianapolis, set a record for the biggest crowd ever to attend an indoor basketball game at 67,500.

"It was an amazing thing to experience that I will never forget."

It certainly was a far cry from playing before a few hundred people at Chapman College in the LPBA or St. Louis' Kiel Auditorium in the WBL.

"Most of the all-star players were from the 1980 Olympic team that boycotted and had also played in the WBL. Unfortunately, I collided with Lynette Woodward (who went on to join the Globetrotters) in the first game and dislocated my left shoulder. Despite my assurances that I was OK, my playing time was limited for the rest of the tour."

Molly remembers Woodward and Teresa Edwards as two of the most noteworthy members of the Olympic team she played against. It was the first of five Olympics for Edwards, who would go on to play in both the American Basketball League and WNBA (where she would also serve as an assistant coach). In 2000, Sports Illustrated ranked her 22nd among the 100 greatest female athletes of the 20th century.

With no basketball league to play in, Molly took part in some clinics, one of which involved promoting a training aid called Hoop-Mate alongside Lakers star forward James Worthy. The orange semicircle attached to the top of the rim on either side, creating an arc that gave shooters a vertical image of the basket and helped them aim more effectively. This helped players target the center of the basket, rather than shooting at the front or back of the rim.

The orange semicircle was originally a bicycle tire, but the designer decided not to pursue the concept further, leaving Clyde Fouts to refine the idea and obtain a patent. A later version created a different sort of target: a small orange orb suspended about a foot above the basket.

Fouts, who had coached at Rosemead High School east of Los Angeles, then tracked statistical data to illustrate how the system worked: by eliminating flat shots and encouraging shooters to hold their follow-through, resulting in a higher-arching trajectory.

Hoop-Mate, she says, "increased my arch on my shot by seeing the visual vertical target over the basket, and I've never made so many dead-center swish shots than when I used this for camps. (Fouts) sold several, but there was no money to manufacture a greater number to get costs down."

Fouts also took part in a Los Angeles-area clinic featuring Molly alongside NBA stars Marques Johnson and Norm Nixon, both of whom had recently been traded to the L.A. Clippers. Also in attendance: legendary UCLA coach John Wooden, who had coach the Bruins to 10 national titles in a 12-year span that also included, at one point, an astonishing 88 consecutive wins.

"Needless to say, I was pretty pumped up because they were there, and I wanted to put on a good show for my demonstration," Molly recalls.

"After going through all the fundamental and technical aspects of shooting, I started demonstrating shooting in close and slowly worked further away from the basket. I had a rebounder and got into a rhythm shooting jump shots, continuing to move further out, then beyond the 3-point line, making nearly every shot.

"Norm and Marques Johnson started high-fiving each other when I made like 12 to15 in a row from long distance, obviously not what they expected to see. John Wooden turned to the coach I attended with, Clyde Fouts, and told him, 'That is best female shooter I've ever seen.'"

Nixon subsequently invited Molly to speak at his basketball camp.

Bill Byrne tries again

By the time the Olympics rolled around, it had been three years since the WBL's demise. But Bill Byrne wasn't ready to give up on the concept of women's pro basketball. On the contrary: One of his big ideas behind the WBL had been tying it to the 1980 Games, which he was counting on to raise the profile of the sport and introduce a nation to a crop of soon-to-be-pro superstars. The Olympic boycott had squelched those hopes.

Dallas Diamonds coach Greg Williams is blunt in his assessment that the boycott all but doomed the WBL. "We were favored to beat the Russians," he says. "Had we won the gold medal, those players would have become household names, and they would have come into the WBL and given it a nice impetus to continue. The boycott was kind of the nail in the coffin for the WBL."

Conversely, however, Team USA's success in the Los Angeles Olympics gave Byrne reason enough to try again.

When the Women's American Basketball Association was formed in April of 1984, Byrne announced teams in Atlanta, Baltimore, Boston (or Milwaukee), Chicago, Columbus, Dallas, Houston, New Jersey and New York for a fall schedule of 22 to 30 games. Byrne said he planned to switch to the summer the following year, adding teams in Denver, Los Angeles, San Francisco and Seattle.

The summer season never came, and the teams in Baltimore, Boston, New York and New Jersey never materialized. A full draft was held, although the Houston team, which turned out to be the worst in the league, was anything but prepared.

Williams, who was set to coach a resurrected version of the

Diamonds, found himself drafting players on behalf of his cross-state rival.

"I'd stayed in touch with Bill Byrne, who had started the WBL and also started the WABA," he says. "I got to the draft, and he told me, 'The Houston franchise can't get a representative there to draft on the first day. Can you do me a favor and draft for them?' I was the head coach for the Dallas Diamonds, and I hadn't even been hired yet!"

Damien, wearing a Minks shirt, guards Molly in a game of one-on-one.

Byrne's attentions, though, were divided. As he was setting up WABA, he was also putting together a $15 million package for a United States Football League team in Columbus. But Byrne wanted to play in Ohio State University's stadium, and the Big Ten Conference didn't allow its members to rent their stadiums to pro teams. The deal never happened.

When the dust settled, Dallas wound up with most of the talent: Lieberman was joined on the Diamonds roster by twins Pam and Paula McGee, fresh off a pair of national championships at USC. Pam would later play two seasons in the WNBA, and two of her children — JaVale and Imani — would be drafted by the NBA and WNBA, respectively.

"We were kind of like the Golden State Warriors then," Williams says. "We had a stacked team."

Byrne called Molly and told her about his plans for the new league in the fall. That was when she flew to Boston to appear in the Spalding commercial with Larry Bird. The tie-in: Spalding was to be the official ball of the WABA. After filming wrapped, she reported to Columbus, where Byrne lived and the new league had its headquarters.

Molly was drafted by the New York franchise, but that team failed to materialize, so Byrne set Molly up with the Columbus club, to be called the Minks. He told her the first season would be a short one — just 22 games compared with 34 or 36 during the WBL days and lasting from just October until the end of the year, which would give him a chance to attract more investors for the second season.

Molly's mother agreed to look after Damien in Southern California while Molly got ready to play in the new league.

"I made arrangements as soon as I could and hopped on a plane to Columbus, Ohio, full of excitement and anticipation," she says. "Someone picked me up from the airport late at night, and then I was dropped off at a dormitory building at Rickenbacker Air Force Base, about 15 miles outside of Columbus."

Winter came early that year, and the air base hadn't turned the heat on yet, so Molly had to run hot water in the shower to warm up her room. But that wasn't the only chill in the air when she arrived: She also got a frosty welcome from her teammates. She didn't know anyone else on the team, or anyone on the coaching staff, for that matter, and the other players gave her the cold shoulder when she arrived for her first practice.

"From the very start of my career, I always got along great with my teammates and was blindsided by the overwhelming feeling of not being welcomed," she says. "There were two or three players that were friendly, so I worked on getting to know the team as quickly as I could so I would be accepted. Angie Paccione from Stanford was very good to me, offering rides in her car to practices and her friendship. The head coach was aloof to me, though the assistant coach, thankfully, was friendly, but I knew I was in an uphill battle to get respect."

Some of her new teammates were reluctant to pass her the ball, and it didn't help when she reinjured the shoulder she'd hurt during the Olympic trials. Meanwhile, the chilly conditions at the air base took on some of her teammates, who began to get sick, so they moved out and checked into hotel rooms in Columbus until contracts could be offered.

When Molly's turn came, the news wasn't good. Molly recalls talk of a large contract for Nancy Lieberman, who was the first player taken in the draft and wound up with the resurrected Dallas Diamonds, but news reports said most of the players would be making in the neighborhood of $6,000 for the season.

"When the coach finally came to my room to make a contract offer, he wrote a number on a piece of paper and slid it over to me. I took a look at it and saw it was close to what I made my first year in Iowa. I said, 'So, this is it?' He said yes, that he had worked out a budget to sign the whole team and this was all he could offer. I told him, 'Thank you for making my decision to go back to California so easy.'

"It was no longer about me anymore — my mom had put her life on hold to help me, and I was missing my son and for what? I finally faced that I was very unhappy, and if I couldn't make any real contributions to the team or make much money, it was no longer worth the sacrifices.

"So, I told Bill Byrne I was leaving, and he put on the full-court press to convince me to stay. He promised to subsidize my income and offered me color commentary jobs with the league games being televised starting with a game coming up in Chicago, which I accepted. But I booked my flight home through Chicago and helped on the broadcast for that game. I told Bill that I had things to take care of before I could commit to staying with the team."

Back in California, Molly caught the flu, and it was a couple of weeks before she could get back to Columbus and rejoin the team.

Byrne, meanwhile, was growing desperate. The nine- or 10-team league he had envisioned started the season with just six franchises, four in the South and two in the Midwest. In addition to the Minks and the Diamonds, the league consisted of the Atlanta Comets, Spirit of Chicago, Houston Shamrocks and Virginia Wave. The Minks won three of their first five games, but they were drawing only a handful of fans to their games. Just 723 showed up for their opener, a 103-98 overtime win over Atlanta, and other games attracted "crowds" of 503 and 251.

"Bill felt they really needed a player like me who could put points on the board," Molly says. "He started calling me daily and promising solutions to all my concerns: income, housing, and not being welcome on the team. He eventually convinced me to meet up with the team in Dallas, and they would have a uniform for me to play. One of the concessions by Bill was to sign my Cornet teammate Doris Draving, and both of us moved into Bill Byrne's house."

With Molly on the court, the Minks started to win, and pretty soon it was clear that the league consisted of Dallas at the top, the Minks on their heels, and everyone else way back in the rear-view mirror. It was a case of the haves and have-nots: In one game, Dallas dismantled rival Houston 103-59.

In fact, the Diamonds had so many good players that Williams ended up platooning them, which meant the stars got less playing time. Lieberman wasn't 100 percent because she was coming off an ankle injury, so Williams played her less than full time. But that didn't sit well with the owner, who fired Williams early into the season ... even though the team was winning its games by an average of 16 points.

"I was fired six games into the season even though we were 6-0 because I wasn't playing the players he wanted to see playing," Williams says. "To my knowledge, I'm the only pro head coach to be fired with a perfect record."

The owner, Ed DuBaj, named himself head coach after sacking Williams — whom he later brought back, only to fire a second time.

But outside of Dallas, few people were showing up for WABA games. The Atlanta Comets' owners pulled out and would have folded a month into the season if DuBaj and Chicago owner Larry Fuhrer hadn't stepped in to prop up the team. In November, seven Atlanta players boycotted a game against Dallas because they hadn't been paid. Only 200 people showed up for that game, and the Comets were averaging no more than 350 fans for their home games.

At the same time they pitched in to keep the Comets from flaming out, DuBaj and Fuhrer also stepped in to help keep the Virginia Wave from crashing.

The highlight of the season was a Nov. 4 game between the Diamonds and the Minks at the Columbus Fairgrounds, featuring a matchup between Molly and Lieberman (highlights of this game were posted on YouTube). Dallas came into the game unbeaten at 10-0, while the Minks stood in second place at 5-2. But Columbus led most of the way, with Molly hitting a number of key jump shots and free throws to keep the Minks ahead en route to a 92-90 upset.

But the Minks eventually collapsed, as well.

"In Columbus, I saw firsthand how hard Bill Byrne worked to make this league viable at the expense of his own health and finances, and his wife was so supportive and kind to us when we were there," Molly says. "I had a new appreciation and understanding of what an amazing feat he had pulled off in forming the WBL. But he was unable to get the finances needed for Columbus, as well as a few other teams.

"Frequently, owners would make a commitment, then reneged when it came time to pay up. The only paycheck I received was on my birthday in November and, with Doris there, it was a day to celebrate. I only played nine games, and when I got injured again with my shoulder, the doctor told me that I had done enough damage and needed to take time off playing to consider surgery. So, I booked my trip home, planning to leave after a home game.

"As workman's comp insurance was required by law, my medical follow up with my shoulder was covered, and I received my entire Columbus Minks salary through my workman's comp payments. It was a real blessing in disguise, because the team continued to struggle financially to the end of the season, and I was the only one to be fully compensated for the season."

Byrne was ultimately ousted as commissioner by DuBaj, whose Diamonds and the Spirit of Chicago were the only two teams still standing at the end of the season. They played for the championship by default — even though Chicago lost more than twice as many games as it won — with the Diamonds, predictably, winning.

DuBaj made some statements about wanting to move the league offices to Dallas and try again in 1985, but nothing ever came of it.

The WABA was officially dead.

One more time

Two years after the collapse of the WABA, Molly found herself involved in her fourth professional basketball league, but unlike the other three, she wasn't going to be involved as a player.

She would be in the front office, as assistant commissioner.

This time, Bill Byrne wasn't involved in the league: It was being run by commissioner Wayne Fulcher, president Ephriam McDaniel and business manager Howard Hanson.

"In about May of 1986, I began getting calls from the organizer of the NWBA, Ephriam McDaniel," Molly says. "He told me how this new concept his group had for a women's pro basketball league was a guaranteed success."

Rather than having separate ownership for each of the eight teams in the circuit, the league would run them all as a single entity, eliminating the potential for bidding wars over popular players. Players would make between $10,000 and $18,000 a year, with a $2,000 bonus available to any player who finished her degree while playing in the league. The regular season would be 48 games — 25 percent longer than the WBL season had been and more than twice as long as the ill-fated WABA.

Ephriam told Molly the league had secured $5 million from investors and was launching a big campaign for a public offering to bring in even more. "Then, once the league was established and on solid ground, each of the teams would be sold as individual franchises, with the original investors getting first options."

Team sites — six of which were in the South — were

chosen because they were places where women's basketball was popular. The clubs all had regional names: the Pride of Iowa would play in Des Moines, the Carolina Blaze in Charlotte, the Texas Twisters in Austin, the Tennessee Tigercats in Knoxville, the Virginia Express in Richmond, the Georgia Peaches in Atlanta, and the Louisiana Blues in Monroe. There would also be a West Coast team, the California Stars, based in Orange County.

The Stars' home was in close proximity to three prominent Olympians from USC: the McGee sisters, who had played for the WABA incarnation of the Dallas Diamonds, and Cheryl Miller, considered by many the premier player in the country. Miller was the top pick in the NWBA draft but never showed any inclination to play for the league.

"I was very interested and liked the creative approach to try things a bit differently to keep a league viable until it took off," Molly says. "I knew it would take several seasons to find the best markets to support a team."

But the big attraction was the idea of returning pro basketball to Iowa. The team, when it was first announced, was to be called the Aces, and the barnstorming theme remained after it changed its name to the Pride: The team logo featured a ponytailed woman, wearing aviator's goggles, riding (or piloting) a giant winged basketball.

Says Molly: "The real hook for me was giving Iowa another shot."

But her role would be different this time, because her priorities had shifted: Instead of wanting to get back on the court, she was looking for the best way to promote women's basketball.

"They wanted me to be involved however I wanted: either as a player, coach, or general manager of a team," she says. "If I was going to get involved again, I wanted to be in a position to use my experience to help the league succeed. After the fiasco with the WABA only two years earlier, I didn't feel that playing or coaching would make much of a difference, so I asked to be the assistant commissioner of the league, and they agreed."

McDaniel asked her to fly out to South Carolina for a meeting, and after staying several days, Molly agreed to participate in a promotional video of the NWBA. She also set up a press conference in Des Moines and invited Iowa's governor, to help lend her credibility in Iowa to the new attempt to establish a women's pro basketball league. However, McDaniel told her that he couldn't pay her ticket to Iowa upfront because they were still in the process of setting up a bank account for the league. She'd be reimbursed for her expenses once everything was in place. This, Molly says, was the first red flag, but she also knew it wasn't unusual for businesses to reimburse people for their expenses, so she bought a $400 airline ticket to make it happen.

"Red flag No. 2: I finally saw the finished video that I had also done a voiceover script for, and it was so bad to be almost laughable," she says. "Not so much the video itself, but the clips inserted from one of the main financial officers talking about what gifts a person would receive for buying a $10 founding member package: T-shirt, a certificate and a cheap medallion 'with a hole punched in the middle so could be worn on a chain.'"

The most news coverage the league ever got was thanks to an August press conference Molly called with the governor of Iowa to announce the new league and the Pride of Iowa team. The league hired former Colorado State head coach Lee Swayze to run the Pride, and signed Barbara Groves on Indiana State and Wendy Bradetich of Michigan to play in Iowa. It had also set its sights on signing Vickie Adkins of Kansas and, most significantly, Wanda Ford from Drake University, who had led the nation in scoring and rebounding the previous year.

But on Aug. 22, Ford announced she had signed with a pro team in Acona, Italy instead. The team had offered her $21,000, which was $3,000 more than the NWBA's top salary, and offered her some stability she feared the new circuit lacked.

"I don't know if the NWBA is going to be successful," she said in announcing her decision. "If I had signed to play and the league folded, I would have missed the opportunity to play in Italy. ... If the NWBA makes it, I'll be back to play in it next year."

News stories about the league trickled out over the next few weeks, and practice sessions opened in late September, with *The Tennessean* in Nashville running a Sept. 28 story headlined: "Women's basketball league begins climb to credibility."

That climb, however, was cut short before it began. Five days after that story appeared, the status of the Pride was called into question when a story revealed the team had only signed six players and hadn't even practiced. An exhibition game scheduled for Oct. 4 had been canceled.

On Oct. 30, Fulcher denied that the league was folding, but admitted that it would have to drop the Texas and California teams to reduce travel costs, along with Iowa, because it had only five players.

Molly, meanwhile, refused to do any more work for the league until it paid her the $400 in travel expenses it owed her.

"I called Ephriam a few more times, and he finally admitted they were struggling, but said he would send me a check from his personal account to pay for my ticket to Iowa," she recalls. "Not surprisingly, the check bounced, and the NWBA, which had started with such promise, never got out of the gate."

The Carolina team was the last to cease operations, and the league officially folded in late January without having played a single game.

"I would like to say that I wished I hadn't gotten involved with the NWBA," Molly says, looking back. "But I believed in the future of women's pro basketball and was always ready to jump in and help, even if there was only the slightest chance of success, so I have no regrets."

A new ballgame

When it became clear another new league wasn't about to make a go of it after the NWBA went belly-up, Molly turned her attention to other pursuits. She became a self-employed painting contractor which gave her the freedom to also work as an instructor at various basketball camps around the country.

"I never pursued coaching myself," she says, "as I was so focused on wanting to get another pro league going. But I loved being an instructor at basketball camps and clinics starting from the time I was 15 to about age 50. Starting with Bob Spencer's camps that I first attended working in the food line, he hired me as a camp counselor to demonstrate drills starting the summer before my junior year of high school, through working at NBA camps to creating my own instructional camps.

"Most of the time, I taught shooting fundamentals and tried to show young aspiring players that you could be an average size person, like myself, and still be successful by learning the fundamentals, putting in the practice time and developing power in your legs."

When Damien was with his father during the summer, she would travel to various locations across the country, running three-day shooting camps for The Shot Doctor, including one in

Centerville, just 12 miles from Moravia. The program was run by Ed Stahl, a 6-foot-10 center who had played at the University of North Carolina, then professionally in Italy. He started the program in 1986 and ran it for 30 years.

"What was cool about my 'having a ball, will travel' days was if I wanted to visit a relative in a certain part of the country, Wyoming for instance, I could call an area coach and set up a one-day shooting clinic and pay for my expenses to get there and donate my Saturday to work with all the kids," Molly says.

In the mid-1990s, Molly worked with Dave Almstead, the former Dallas Diamonds president, on an idea for a "Short Court" 3-on-3 women's tournament. The Liberty Sports cable network was looking for more programming, and the idea seemed on the verge of becoming reality.

Molly described the concept in a fact sheet as "an all-female tournament with a unique twist." The game would be played on a smaller court, 45 feet long by 30 feet wide, with players from the 1996 Olympic team, European leagues and recent college graduates competing for prize money. A clinic for kids, conducted by the players, was also planned.

"It is a festive, upbeat and fast-paced event that takes the game of basketball outdoors the way the Pro Beach Volleyball Circuit took the game of volleyball outdoors," the fact sheet read.

Games would last 20 minutes under normal rules, but without free throws "to keep the action going." The tournament was to be played in Palm Desert on a weekend in October 1996.

Unfortunately, two things kept the tournament from happening. First, not one but two new women's pro leagues — the American Basketball League and WNBA — announced the intention to begin competing around the same time. Second, Liberty was bought out by Fox Sports, which shelved the idea.

"While timing is always an important element in determining how things happen, in television the single most important element is always the ability to find financial sponsorship to underwrite the production costs," Almstead says. "Molly's proposal got caught in the transition and growth of the Regional Sports Networks (RSN's) — read that consolidation of the RSN's. Against the backdrop of the RSN consolidation, the emergence of the NBA's plans for the WNBA and the inability to find sponsorship support, the 3-on-3 cable tournament never got off the ground."

Molly offers instruction at a camp after her playing days.

Giving Back

Molly continued to work with kids across the country to teach and share her shooting techniques in many basketball camps in clinics. Together with her husband John Kazmer, they formed Shot Camp Academy and developed many basketball programs for kids in their community including the YMCA, the Boys and Girls Cub, and Park and Recreation Department.

In 1989, Molly married John, who has played basketball for Hall of Fame coaches Jerry Tarkanian and Lute Olson at Long Beach State, which rose to No. 2 in the nation in the early 1970s. The 6-foot-4 swingman went on to play professionally overseas, including with a team in the Philippines, before returning to the United States and settling in the Palm Springs area, east of Los Angeles.

After his playing career ended, he became general manager of the Palm Springs Mall, but also stayed active in the game, serving as an assistant coach at Palm Desert and La Quinta high schools.

"John and I got married when Damien was 11, and John has a daughter Michelle a couple of years younger than him — so we had a blended family, and we added two redheads, Casey and Kenzie."

Although both Molly and John had played pro basketball, it was another sport — softball — that brought them together. Molly joined a fast-pitch women's softball league shortly after moving to Palm Springs in 1987, and around the same time, also started playing in a slow-pitch coed league. John was going through a divorce at the time, and his neighbor invited him to play on the team, as well. (He'd actually been a baseball player before taking up basketball, having grown a foot over the summer as a teenager.)

"He had also played some high-level softball leagues and didn't think playing with women on the team would be very competitive, but he needed to get out of the house, so he joined," Molly says. "He had no idea what he was getting into because the girls on that coed team could really play!

John had a strong arm, so he played left field, with Molly at second base.

"One time in practice, he threw a ball to me to tag a runner, but it was like a high arc because he didn't want to throw it too hard at me. I was quite disgusted at not being able to tag the runner out, so when he walked back to the outfield I threw the ball at his back and said, 'Next time, *throw* the damn ball!

"The next time the same situation came up as the runner headed to second, he took his time fielding it then threw the ball as hard as he could just inches off the ground. I snagged it and tagged the runner out and pointed at him and said, 'Now, *that's* a throw!' And according to him, that's when he was smitten."

The pair remained fiercely competitive as their relationship blossomed.

"In the early days, almost everything we did turned into a competition — including basketball in the driveway," Molly says. "When he would go in for a dunk, I would shove him against the garage door to stop him and just say, 'Foul.' So, he would have to shoot from almost the street to beat me — which he could, but at least I made him work for it."

Paying it forward

"One of the most rewarding things is life is being able to use your talents to help others," Molly says. "Many of the pioneers in the WBL have gone on to make major contributions both to basketball and society in general."

After her playing days with the ended, Cornets point guard Robin Tucker served as head women's basketball coach at Florida Atlantic University from 1984 to 1987 and was named the Converse Coach of the Year during her tenure. Later, she became a physical education teacher at Beacon Elementary School in Hilliard, Ohio.

While there, she was instrumental in closing down a toxic and hazardous waste disposal company next to the school. She also helped raise more than $20,000 through "basketball shoot-outs" to help defray the medical expenses for the children near the school who were diagnosed with leukemia. Tucker has also been involved in improving conditions for the elderly in nursing homes and rehabilitation facilities.

Tanya Crevier has continued performing since her WBL days, and her enthusiastic spintacular basketball show has taken her all over the world, including 35 countries and all 50 states. She has brought smiles to countless faces while performing at schools, camps, prisons, nursing homes and major sporting events. A member of the South Dakota Sports Hall of Fame, she continues to showcase her amazing skills of ballhandling, spinning and juggling basketballs while sharing her message of hope and inspiration with young and old alike.

After she finished playing, Doris Draving worked in physical therapy and taught school at the Albuquerque Academy. She utilized her athletic skills by coaching basketball, volleyball, softball and swimming. She was the athletic director for 16 years at a Catholic school in Florida.

Cardte Hicks, who played alongside Molly on the San Francisco Pioneers, has been running a program that provides support to schools in dealing with bullying and cultural differences. Legends-Kids First, Inc. empowers individuals, families and communities to build healthy lifestyles and productive lives, offering guidance, tools, and support to achieve their potential.

One of Molly's rewarding opportunities came when she and John were offered a chance to develop an afterschool program for Palm Desert Middle School.

"We were in the process of setting up a club basketball program when we were invited to speak at Palm Desert Middle School by one of the parents of a student in our program. It was 'Career Day,' and parents came to the school to talk about and inspire young students on various career options. John and I each gave presentations about playing pro basketball to about four different classes, and by the end of the day, the word was out that we were a big hit with the kids."

The principal called the Kazmers in with news that the school would be receiving a city grant for an on-campus afterschool program, and asked whether they would be interested in developing and directing it. That was the genesis of their Shot Camp Academy afterschool program, which began with a dozen sixth- through eighth-grade students in 2007.

Basketball was just a small part of the curriculum. Molly came up with activities and exercises including arts and crafts, sign language, square dancing, photography, Wiffle Ball, dodgeball, football and, of course, basketball. A teacher who had spent time in Japan helped out with instruction on Japanese culture.

Meanwhile, Molly and John lent financial support to the school's robotics and dance programs.

"Our program was set up to provide afterschool tutoring and enrichment programs, and we based it on the character-building concepts we used with our basketball programs," Molly says. "We began tracking grades and made dramatic improvements from each quarter by identifying what each student needed help with."

The original group of 12 students quickly multiplied to more than 100 as word about the program spread.

"It was a good thing that John had a talent for controlling large groups," Molly says. "It was a low-cost program thanks to the city grant, but we frequently brought kids in that were unable to pay anything, often on the recommendation from the guidance counselors.

"We ran the program with great success for five years and were able to make a positive impact on the lives of over 700 kids that went through our program during that time. When our kids went on to high school, they would often come back to visit or help out. This was without a doubt one of the most rewarding jobs I've had in my life, and we still run into our students from time to time who will run across the mall to say 'hi' when they spot us. It was amazing to have the opportunity to introduce our 'basketball values' to hundreds of kids who didn't even play sports."

Molly got her real estate license in 2001 but only worked part time during the five years she and John ran their afterschool program, from 2007 to 2012, when she joined her current company.

"I love the freedom, and my competitiveness from my past has definitely helped me find a way to get the most difficult deals done," she says. "Most of the time it's very rewarding, and I've had great clients become friends. I was a stay-at-home mom with my two younger kids from 1992 to 2000, as I was never again going to miss what I missed with Damien."

Going home again

Molly was inducted into the Iowa High School Basketball Hall of Fame in 1986, and in 1998, she attended the opening of an exhibit on women's pro basketball at the Basketball Hall of Fame in Springfield, Mass. She was featured prominently in a display that included her warmup suit, a Cornets pennant and a cardboard cutout of her getting ready to shoot.

The following year, she was inducted into the Grand View College Athletic Hall of Fame, and in 2018, the WBL as a league was installed in the Women's Basketball Hall of Fame as "Trailblazers of the Game."

Former WBL players inducted as individuals include Carol Blazejowski, Nancy Lieberman, Ann Meyers and Lusia Harris, each of whom was recognized with the inaugural class of 1999. WBL alumni inducted in subsequent years include Holly Warlick, Muffet McGraw, Nancy Dunkle, Inge Nissen, Patricia Roberts, Rosie Walker, Tara Heiss, Cindy Brogdon, Pearl

The Legend of Molly Bolin

Moore and Peggie Gillom. Carolyn Bush Roddy, who played for the Dallas Diamonds, was voted in as a 2019 inductee.

But despite her scoring records, her back-to-back championship appearances and her 1979-80 MVP award, Molly's name isn't on that list.

One of her most treasured honors, however, occurred in 2012, when she was invited back to Moravia for an assembly in her honor to celebrate her inclusion in the school's Wall of Fame.

Referencing Bon Jovi's *Who Says You Can't Go Home*, Molly says there's only one place they call her one of their own.

Molly at her induction into the Iowa High School Basketball Hall of Fame in 1986.

"For me, that's Moravia, Iowa."

She's still in touch with Carolyn Woodward, whose daughter, Regina, was Molly's best friend in childhood and who still lives in Moravia, having "adopted her" when her own mother passed away. The small town in south-central Iowa is about the same size it was when Molly went to school, twirled batons and befriended raccoons there. It's not only where Molly grew up, it played a big part in who she became: the most successful women's basketball player ever to come out of the Hawkeye State.

"When basketball faded out of my life, I mostly looked the other way because it was too painful to watch," she says. "So now and then over the years I would lose touch with who I am, and all it would take is a trip back to my hometown of Moravia or a call to Carolyn Woodward, to get back on track."

Molly has been back to Moravia plenty of times, but the 2012 trip was special. The May 1 edition of the *Moravia Union* carried the lead headline "Welcome Home Molly!" There's even a mural in town that shows her shooting a basketball. It's on the side of the first brick building as you head into town.

Looking back, she credits her Moravia upbringing as being foundational to her success.

"Growing up learning small-town Midwest values and the determination to compete and succeed in sports shaped me into the person I am," she says. Being unspoiled and unentitled as the fifth of six kids in my family, I was more than willing to work for what I wanted."

Another ingredient in her success: the 6-on-6 style of basketball that many people thought put girls at a disadvantage when they left high school. In fact, three girls would file a lawsuit in 1983, contending that Iowa's style of play hurt their chances of playing in college. A decade later, the state dropped the format, making the switch to the five-person game.

But for Molly, the result was just the opposite.

"It's so ironic that the game that was ended for 'equality' to compete for college scholarships was a huge part of what set me apart from many great players of my era," she says. "If I hadn't grown up in Iowa, and more specifically in Moravia, with a winning tradition and sellout crowd support, *and* the golden opportunity to earn my way to a basketball camp, I'm sure my path would have been very different."

"Learning to create a shot with only one or two dribbles and having the chance to shoot so much in 32 minutes — because of the quick transition of the ball being passed by refs from one end after a made basket to center court — put me way ahead of the curve offensively after stepping into the college and pro levels.

"It never really hit me, until I read the Steph Curry article, how much my Iowa roots came into play in my pro career. I'm sure nobody thought playing the 6-on-6 game could turn out to be a huge advantage for a player but it *was*! Looking back, it's almost overwhelming to see the level of talent that played in the WBL and that I competed against, including many all-time greats, and I have to give a lot of credit to my Iowa upbringing."

Molly has a different life now than the one she lived in the past, but that past shaped who she is today. The competitive drive to be the best on the basketball court has served her well in real estate, too. And her desire to give back to the game that means so much to her means thousands of youngsters have benefited from her example.

One of those kids is Damien, who boasted a 4.0 grade-point average and set the Palm Desert High School high jump record at 6 feet, 9 inches. He also played basketball, and John was on the coaching staff when his team won the Desert Valley League Championship his senior year.

John and Damien would spend hours dunking on the 9-foot baskets at an elementary school near their house before Damien graduated and headed off to college.

"He started college at the beach area, but after his roommate left, he ended up going back to Iowa to college and stayed there after a brief time in Florida, working for my brother."

Today, "Damien is married, has his MBA and works in Des Moines with two daughters and a stepson. We stay in touch, though I only get to see them about once a year. He rarely sees Dennie, who still lives in Moravia."

Daughter Kenzie earned a Division II volleyball scholarship to Black Hills State University in South Dakota. Damien drove in from Iowa, and the entire family gathered to watch her last match, which she clinched with a kill from the outside. She earned all-conference honors for the 16-team Rocky Mountain Athletic Conference.

Molly's father, meanwhile, was able to get control of his drinking and put an end to his abusive behavior.

"My little brother hunted and fished with my dad and was too young to remember the worst times, and they had a good relationship," she says. "I did, too, for the most part, and he was very supportive of my basketball career when he realized I was in the papers all the time. I know he was proud — though he wasn't one to say so.

"As an adult, I understand what happened and was able to forgive and let it go a long time ago. I think my mom taught all four of us girls not to ever put up with abuse (by seeing what happens when you *do* tolerate it) and we are all pretty feisty that way."

Molly's father was diagnosed with cancer in 1990, and the following June, she returned to Iowa for a visit. Her plane was delayed, and she arrived to find her father waiting for her in the car, hooked up to an oxygen tank.

"I remember getting in the front seat of the car with him and saying, 'Why the hell are you driving?' He said it was easier for him to travel when he drove, but he did not look good and his color was grayish. We drove another two or three hours to my sister's house in Nebraska from the airport, and that night as we were getting ready to go to bed, he collapsed and died. I had recently taken CPR classes, so I worked on him until the ambulance got there, but later they told me he died right away and there was nothing I could have done."

She stayed in Moravia for a couple of weeks and helped clean out the house for a big auction sale. Within a couple of years, her mother had moved out to California near Molly.

Molly's mom, Wanda, who was always her number one fan — and had made herself Molly's "unofficial press secretary" — always sending updates on Molly's career to the Iowa newspapers, passed away in 2006.

Legacy

Many outside of Moravia have forgotten about Molly's achievements. The WBL lasted just three years, and the passage of time can dim the memories of those who may have read about her exploits in the sports pages four decades ago.

But that doesn't diminish her contribution to the game as a record-setting scorer and one of the first players to perfect the modern jump shot. To those who saw her play, the memories remain vivid.

She's often remembered by fans for "her most accurate shot and her attractive looks," as Doris Draving puts it. But Draving and others who knew her well during her playing days also recall her upbeat demeanor and dedication to the game.

"As a teammate, she was positive and was always encouraging," Draving says, and Carolyn Woodward of Moravia recalls that, even as a child, "she was never afraid of hard work."

"Molly always had a smile on her face and was well liked by everyone," Cornets assistant Bruce Mason says. "The thing a lot of people didn't see about Molly was how hard working she was. She practiced shooting hours upon hours to make herself the best player she could be. Her deceptive first step and her ability to pull up and shoot the jump shot made her the outstanding player that she was."

Robin Tucker points out that, "because Molly did not play for a major university ... before entering the WBL, she never got the respect or the awards that she deserved. Molly had the best one- or two-dribble drive and step-back jumper I had ever seen. She had a high release and could shoot over anyone assigned to guard her."

Dave Almstead, former president of the Dallas Diamonds, described her as "a fearless shooter" who "really had a grittiness about the way she played" and was "always high energy."

Diamonds coach Greg Williams says, even though the game has evolved, Molly would have had no problem playing in the modern WNBA. She was a great shooter," he says. "She was very active offensively — she was always on the move — and she had a quick release. There were not a lot of players back then who could create their own shot off the dribble. She was like a George Gervin, Ray Allen-type of player that you can't leave open.

"Molly had great off-the-ball movement, which is pretty amazing because this was back in the era when a lot of teams didn't play 5-on-5. They played just 3-on-3 in the front court, and that was Molly's background coming into the pro league. But you could tell she had a high basketball I.Q. She was just a pleasure to watch, just as a pure basketball fan."

The only reason Molly isn't in the Hall of Fame, Williams says, is the fact that not enough people around today actually saw what she could do: "I guarantee you, if they could see Molly play live and in person, she'd be in."

A player ahead of her time, her playing days were numbered by the lack of opportunities. The year she set the

The Legend of Molly Bolin

WBL scoring records and was the MVP, she would have been a senior in college had she not turned pro.

Along with the lasting scoring records she set at Moravia High School and while playing for the Iowa Cornets, Molly should be remembered, along with the rest of the Hall of Fame WBL Trailblazers, for their ultimate efforts and sacrifices to pave the way for women's professional basketball. The WNBA is enjoying its 21st season and televised games — something the WBL could only dream of.

Today, Molly continues to promote women's basketball, serving as a board member of Legends of the Ball. This organization is dedicated to preserving the history of the WBL by showcasing its connection to the growth of women's basketball at every level.

Molly never gave up on believing in the future of women's pro basketball, playing in three pro leagues and trying to help two others get off the ground before the WNBA announced its formation in 1996. Her contributions and dedication to the game, even beyond her playing days, have created the lasting legacy of The Legend of Molly Bolin.

LEGENDS OF THE BALL, INC.
"Passing it on...Paying it Forward"

The WBL Effect...

512-270-8232
legendsoftheball@lobinc.org
🐦 @legends_lobinc

By the Numbers

50-point games, Moravia HS			
Points	**Opponent**	**Score**	**Date**
83	Leon	97-55	Jan. 21, 1975
76	Seymour	101-73	Jan. 10, 1975
70	Lamoni	92-74	Dec. 5, 1973
70	Mormon Trail	94-95 (L)	Feb. 11, 1975
69	Mormon Trail	79-77	Jan. 14, 1975
68	Pella Christian	102-72	Nov. 26, 1974
65	Wayne Community	82-68	Jan. 18, 1974
65	Centerville (sectional final)	81-52	Feb. 19, 1974
64	Wayne (district semifinal)	84-85 (L)	Feb. 23, 1974
63	Centerville	85-73	Nov. 13, 1973
63	Albia	96-68	Nov. 15, 1974
63	Moulton	101-70	Jan. 28,1975
61	Seymour	112-79	Feb. 7, 1975
60	Pella Christian	102-72	Nov. 26, 1974
60	Southeast Warren	78-56	Jan. 7, 1975
59	Mormon Trail	73-64	Jan. 22, 1974
59	Mormon Trail	81-71	Dec. 4, 1974
58	Southeast Warren	102-75	Dec. 2, 1974
57	Chariton	71-69	Jan. 29, 1974
56	Lamoni	79-59	Jan. 15, 1974
56	Southeast Warren	72-51	Feb. 4, 1975
54	Leon	109-62	Dec. 13, 1974
53	Leon	93-58	Jan. 11, 1974
53	Lamoni	78-73	Jan. 26, 1974
53	Lamoni	87-88 (L-2OT)	Dec. 17, 1974
51	Leon	68-48	Nov. 30, 1973
51	Chariton (sectional final)	74-79 (L)	Feb. 25, 1975
50	Centerville	87-73	Nov. 12, 1974
50	Melcher-Dallas	74-44	Jan. 17, 1975
50	Lamoni	83-71	Jan. 24, 1975

Molly's MVP season			
Date	**Opponent**	**Score**	**Points**
Nov. 18	California	124-86	38
Nov. 25	@ Milwaukee	89-88	25
Nov. 27	Chicago	122-111	44
Dec. 2	Washington	97-88	31
Dec. 8	Houston	113-96	19
Dec. 12	Philadelphia	92-85	27
Dec. 13	@ Dallas	99-107 (L)	18
Dec. 15	San Francisco	107-81	37
Dec. 16	New Jersey	100-108 (L)	42
Dec. 27	@ St. Louis	106-115 (L)	42
Dec. 28	Milwaukee	102-94	30
Dec. 30	Dallas	125-93	26
Jan. 3	@ New York	101-109 (L)	27
Jan. 4	@ Chicago	115-114	26
Jan. 7	New Orleans	113-92	38
Jan. 11	San Francisco	90-87	29
Jan. 13	Minnesota	109-103	54
Jan. 17	@ Houston	132-108	29
Jan. 19	@ New Jersey	95-111 (L)	34
Jan. 27	@ Minnesota	93-88	21
Feb. 3	@ New Orleans	91-110 (L)	37
Feb. 4	@ Minnesota	82-97 (L)	35
Feb. 7	@ St. Louis	107-97	47
Feb. 9	@ California	112-115 (L)	25
Feb. 11	@ San Francisco	87-95 (L)	21
Feb. 16	@ Minnesota	104-106 (L)	38
Feb. 17	St. Louis	90-80	26
Feb. 21	New York	131-125	41
Feb. 22	@ Chicago	119-121 (L)	30
Feb. 24	@ New Jersey	103-112 (L)	17
Feb. 28	Milwaukee	102-76	32
March 2	Minnesota	125-85	55
March 3	Chicago	117-83	28
March 6	@ St. Louis	106-87	34
March 9	St. Louis	101-81	40
March 16	@ Milwaukee	106-73	36

The Legend of Molly Bolin

Career highlights

Moravia High School

- Set several school scoring records that still stand
- Single game high of **83** points
- Season scoring average of **54.8**
- Season total points **1,370**
- Scored over **70** points in one game five times
- Selected as a High School All-American

Inducted into Iowa Basketball Hall of Fame

Grand View College

- Led team to Small College National Tournament
- Set a single game school record of **42** points
- First player to score over **1,000** points

Elected to Grand View College Athletic Hall of Fame

Professional

- First player signed to a contract with the first team (Iowa) in the first women's professional basketball league, the WBL (three seasons)
- Three times selected to both the All-Star and the All-Pro teams
- Played in the League's Championship Finals twice
- Led the league in scoring with a record setting **32.8** points per game
- Selected once as the WBL's Most Valuable Player with Ann Meyers
- Set multiple scoring records including:

    Most points in one game – **55**

    Most points in one half – **38**

    Most points in one season – **1,179**

    Highest playoff average – **33.1**

    Most points in playoff game – **50**
- Played in three women's pro leagues and spent 10 years promoting a future for women's pro basketball in the U.S. prior to the WNBA
- Selected to a USA All-Star team to tour against the gold medal-winning 1984 U.S. Olympic Basketball Team
- Served as an instructor at camps and clinics since high school
- Appeared in training videos, commercials and clinics for John Wooden, Pete Newell, Larry Bird and various NBA teams

References

"3 WBL crowns for Cornets; win game, too," Des Moines Register, p. 4S,
    March 17, 1980.

"10 things you never knew about that iconic Farrah Fawcett poster," metv.com,
    Aug. 7, 2018.

"$250,000 budget for Iowa pro team," Des Moines Tribune, p. 21, Feb. 23, 1978.

Alson, Peter. "The Shot Doctor is happy to make house calls," si.com, Jan. 8, 1990.

Ariail, Cat. "Steph Curry ... The 'Male Machine Gun Molly'? Gender and Styles of Play in
    Modern Basketball," Sport in American History, ussporthistory.com, May 12, 2016.

Blackman, Frank. "Bolin's move helps Pioneers," S.F. Examiner, p. F5, March 26, 1981.

Blackman, Frank. "Pioneers given belated Oscar," S.F. Examiner, p. F1, April 1, 1981.

"Bolin boosts Iowa Cornets," Quad-City Times, p. 8, Jan. 8, 1980.

"Bolin leads Cornet win," Iowa City Press-Citizen, p. 2B, April 8, 1980.

"Bolin's 42 help Viking women edge Cyclones," D.M. Register, p. 2S, Feb. 1, 1978.

Bondy, Filip. "The blonde and the beautiful," New York Daily News, p. 48, Feb. 3, 1986.

Bradley, Mark. "7 Comets miss game in protest of failure to receive paycheck,"
    Atlanta Constitution, p. 3-C, Nov. 21, 1984.

"Brutal Winter of 1978-79," weather.gov.

Burdick, Chuck. "Denise Long," D.M. Register, data.desmoinesregister.com.

Carr, Janis. "Bolin (47 Points) Sparks Breeze," L.A. Times, pt. III, p. 7, Dec. 17, 1980.

Carr, Janis. "Breeze to Face Flames," L.A. Times, pt. III, p. 10, Dec. 16, 1980.

Carr, Janis. "What's New? Bolin Scores 40," L.A. Times, pt. III, p. 25, Dec. 12, 1980.

"Coach DeLap's Book," Peach Baskets, coachdelap.wordpress.com.

"Cornets fall in overtime," Des Moines Tribune, p. 9, Feb. 3, 1979.

"Cornets fall short of WBL title," Des Moines Register, p. 1S, May 2,1979.

"Cornets outhustled; Green hit by auto," Des Moines Tribune, p. 18, April 11, 1979.

"Cornets sign 3 to cage pacts," Des Moines Register, p. 23, July 7, 1978.

"Cornets trip Chicago, gain tie for first," Des Moines Register, p. 2S, March 31, 1979.

"Custody battle over Molly's son rocks her home town," Des Moines Register, p. 2B,
    Dec. 5, 1982.

Dyer, Bob. "Iowa's Bolin signs with new league," Des Moines Register, p. S1,
    Sept. 25, 1980.

Dyer, Bob. "Molly," Des Moines Register, p. 1S, Nov. 13, 1979.

"Elizabeth Cambage breaks WNBA scoring record with 53-point game," cbsnews.com,
    July 17, 2018.

Elliiott, Stephen. "Remember when the snows came in 1979?" qconline, Jan. 10, 2007.

Festle, Mary Jo. "Playing Nice: Politics and Apologies in Women's Sports,"

Columbia University Press, New York, 1996.

"FMC Girls Victorious In Tournament Play," Florence (S.C.) Morning News, p. 1, March 24, 1976.

"Ford will sign with Italian pros," Iowa City Press-Citizen, p. 1B, Aug. 23, 1986.

"Freshman-sophomore girls over Moulton-Udell," Moravia Union, p. 4, Dec. 16, 1971.

Fussman, Cal. "Duel at Kiel: Streak Wins Molly-Liz Show," St. Louis Post-Dispatch, p. 4C, Dec. 28, 1979.

Fussman, Cal. "Streak's Whiz Is A Wow: 50 Points," St. Louis Post-Dispatch, p. 1F, Dec. 20, 1979.

"Gems Secure Playoff Berth," Morristown (N.J.) Daily Record, p. 14, March 9, 1981.

"Gems Tip SF For Third Straight," Morristown (N.J.) Daily Record, p. 17, Jan. 13, 1981.

"Girls Basketball Nigh Here Tuesday When Molly Hits 83 Points, and Boys Avenge A Losing Streak," Moravia Union, p. 1, Jan. 23, 1975.

"Girls Lose Heartbreaker By One To Wayne," Moravia Union, p. 1, Feb. 28, 1974.

Goodall, Fred. "WBL Signees Optimistic," Tampa Tribune, p. 5-C, June 24, 1978.

"Grand View Gals Make Transition," Des Moines Tribune, p. 12, Jan. 27, 1976.

"Grand View girls team to national in Ohio," Moravia Union, p. 1, March 11, 1976.

"Grand View loses, not enough players," Waterloo Courier, p. 54, March 16, 1975.

"Grand View wins, 78-66," Des Moines Register, p. 11D, Nov. 16, 1975.

"Grand View women in meet final," Des Moines Register, p. 7D, Nov. 30, 1975.

"Grand View's women romp," Des Moines Register, p. 2S, Nov. 22, 1975.

Grett, Wayne. "All's rosy for WBL, Cornets – sort of," Des Moines Tribune, p. 15, April 16, 1979.

Grett, Wayne. "Bolin's 55 break mark; Cornets win," Des Moines Tribune, p. 3S, March 3, 1980.

Grett, Wayne. "Bolin's back on court at San Francisco," Des Moines Tribune, p. 17, Jan. 8, 1981.

Grett, Wayne. "Bolin scores big in new cage loop: $30,000," Des Moines Tribune, p. 21, Sept, 25, 1980.

Grett, Wayne. "Bolin skids, then sparks late surge," Des Moines Register, p. 4S, Dec. 3, 1979.

Grett, Wayne. "Cagers Coates, Aswegan Lost To Grand View," Des Moines Tribune, p. 33, Sept. 1, 1976.

Grett, Wayne. "Cornets breeze in opener," Des Moines Tribune, p. 19, Nov. 19, 1979.

Grett, Wayne. "Cornets force 5th playoff game," Des Moines Register, p. 1S, April 27, 1979.

Grett, Wayne. "Cornets' rally bags crown, 118-117," Des Moines Register, p. 8D, April 15, 1979.

Grett, Wayne. "Cornets survive clash of leaders," Des Moines Register, p. 2S, March 5, 1979.

The Legend of Molly Bolin

Grett, Wayne. "New Iowa Cornets set to negotiate with 6 or 7 women cagers," Des Moines Tribune p. 17, June 21, 1978.

Grett, Wayne. "Fledgling Iowa Cornets to be movie stars, too," Des Moines Tribune, p. 19, June 29, 1978.

Grett, Wayne. "Ford eyes team in Italy, would pass up U.S. league," Des Moines Register, p. 4S, Aug. 22, 1986.

Grett, Wayne. "Future is bleak for Cornets," Des Moines Tribune, p. 21, Sept. 11, 1980.

Grett, Wayne. "Huge money woes silence Cornets," Des Moines Tribune, p. 15, Sept. 30, 1980.

Grett, Wayne. "Magnificent Molly makes her mark," Des Moines Register, p. 2S, Jan. 14, 1980.

Grett, Wayne. "Meyers leads Gems by Cornets, 108-100," Des Moines Register, p. 4S, Dec. 17, 1979.

Grett, Wayne. "Stars stop Cornets for WBL title," Des Moines Register, p. 31, April 10, 1980.

Grett, Wayne. "WBL boss: If league to survive, promotion 'a must,'" Des Moines Tribune, p. 17, April 14, 1980.

Grett, Wayne. "Record 54 by Bolin! But coach pans effort," Des Moines Tribune, p. 17, Jan. 14, 1980.

Grett, Wayne. "Status of Pride of Iowa in new NWBA unclear," Des Moines Register, p. 27, Oct. 3, 1986.

Grett, Wayne. "Vance out as owner of WBL Cornets," Des Moines Register, p. 33, March 20, 1980.

Grett, Wayne. "What Slump? Bolin hits 40," Des Moines Tribune, p. 13, Jan. 29, 1973.

Grett, Wayne and Fanlund, Paul. "Newcomer Lifts Lincoln," Des Moines Tribune, p. 2-S, Dec. 11, 1973.

Hambleton, Ken. "NU women basketballers hang on to win, 84-81," Lincoln Journal Star, p. 2E, Dec. 4, 1977.

"Harris fires New Jersey past Cornets," Des Moines Register, p. 4S, Feb. 25, 1980.

Hawkins, Chuck. "Vance, team sued over trip," Des Moines Tribune, p. 31, April 30, 1980.

"In Re Marriage of Bolin," Justitia US Law, law.justia.com, July 20, 1983.

"Iowa Cornets first to hire coach," Iowa City Press-Citizen, p. 1B, March 30, 1978.

"Iowa women lost 112-53 to Grand View," Iowa City Press-Citizen," p. 2B, Dec. 10, 1975.

"Iowa women stroll, 88-73," Des Moines Register, p. 22, Nov. 23, 1977.

Jauss, Bill. "Rebounders put Hustle in good position," Chicago Tribune, pt. 6, p. 2, April 6, 1979.

"Joyce Elder Shifts to Grand View," Des Moines Tribune, p. 29, June 25, 1975.

"Jr. High Girls Lose Just One Game," Moravia Union, p. 1, Feb. 11, 1971.

"Junior high teams win from Russell Saturday," Moravia Union, p. 1, Jan. 14, 1971.

"Junior Musicians In Solo Contest," Moravia Union, p. 1, Feb. 20, 1969.

"Kansas State Tops SMS Cage Meet," Springfield News-Leader, p. 11, Dec. 1, 1975.

Kiley, Mike. "Hustle Fans cheer Fincher's playing form, and more," Chicago Tribune, pt. 4, p. 3, April 1, 1979.

Kruse, Don. "Women's pro cage lead on the line in UNI-Dome," Waterloo Courier, p. 14, Jan. 12, 1979.

Lackey, Patrick. "C.R. takes a shot at the silver screen," Des Moines Register, p. 1B, Sept. 11, 1978.

Lamberto, Nick. "Moguls ogle local yokels; flix depix girls' basketball," Des Moines Register, p. 2B, March 24, 1978

Leavitt, Paul. "Court cautions Iowans in Bolin custody ruling," Des Moines Register, p. 1, July 21, 1983.

Leiker, Ken. "Owner folds Flames; possible buyer found," Arizona Republic, p. 3, Dec. 24, 1980.

"Lewis and Bolin lead Cornet win," Waterloo Courier, p. 16, Nov. 26, 1979.

Lewis, Pete. "5 on squad: Vikings win game, 73-34," Des Moines Register, p. 3S, March 15, 1975.

"Little Mohawks split at Blakesburg," Moravia Union, p. 1, Dec. 9, 1971.

Lough, Michael A. "Official Denies Report That Women's League Folding," Alexandria (La.) Town Talk, p. B-2, Oct. 30, 1986.

Maly, Phil. "Talent Galore For Grand View Women Cagers," p. 33, Nov. 13, 1975.

Maly, Ron. "Iowa-made 'Dribble': A 'fun' movie," Des Moines Register, p. 1S, Aug. 29, 1978.

Maly, Ron. "Nissen gambling on women cagers," Des Moines Register, p. 1S, March 22, 1978.

Maly, Ron. "Oh, Sister! Cornets sail in debut," Des Moines Register, p. 2S, Dec. 16, 1978.

Maly, Ron. "On court and on film, Cornets dribble on," Des Moines Register, p. 22, Jan. 27, 1979.

Maly, Ron. "WBL playing games, not basketball," Des Moines Register, p. 27, Feb. 9, 1979.

Martinez, Rick. "Flames open season with big-league loss," Arizona Republic, p. E4, Dec. 13, 1980.

"MHS Boys Have Thrilling Game Here; Girls Win Again With Big Margin," Moravia Union, p. 1, Dec. 16, 1971.

"MHS Girls Just Three Points Short of 'Sweet Sixteen,'" Moravia Union, p. 1, March 1, 1973.

"MHS girls lost to Colfax last week," Moravia Union, p. 1, Jan. 4, 1973.

"MHS girls take second in district again," Moravia Union, p. 1, Feb. 27, 1975.

"Milwaukee Does fire Klinzing as coach," San Bernardino Sun, p. D-3, Dec. 15, 1978.

The Legend of Molly Bolin

"Mohawkettes Snow Leon 109-62 Friday," Moravia Union, p. 1, Dec. 19, 1974.

"Molly Bolin expects homecoming of sorts," Sioux City Journal, p. A16, March 29, 1979.

"Molly Van Benthuysen at basketball camp," Moravia Union, p. 1, Aug. 5, 1971.

"Moravia split victories with Seymour," Moravia Union, p. 2, Dec. 16, 1971.

Muskat, Carrie. "Grand View edges Luther in tourney," Des Moines Tribune, Feb. 24, 1978.

Nelson, Kathleen. "Women's Professional Basketball Tries Again," St. Louis Post-Dispatch, p. 3D, Aug. 14, 1986.

"Nicodemus fired by Does," Appleton (Wis.) Post-Crescent, p. B-6, Jan. 26, 1979.

Naughton, John. "The Register's list of the 50 best Iowa high school girls' basketball stars of all time," Des Moines Register, Feb. 23, 2018.

Nelson, Valerie J. "George Nissen dies at 96; inventor of the modern trampoline," L.A. Times, April 10, 2010.

"New gals' league learning from old one," Indianapolis Star, pt. 4, p. 17, Nov. 2, 1980.

"New Jersey too much for Cornets," Des Moines Register, p. 4D, Jan. 20, 1980.

"New Switch When Boys Win, Girls Lose In Games Here Tuesday Night," Moravia Union, p. 1, Feb. 13, 1975.

"Nicodemus fired before year starts," Lincoln Journal Star, p. 13, Dec. 12, 1978.

Offenburger, Chuck. "Meet supporter of the Cornets," Des Moines Register, p. 1B, Nov. 29, 1979.

"Omaha to get coach of troubled Cornets?" Lincoln Journal Star, p. 4E, July 6, 1980.

"Perfect attendance for first semester at elementary school," Moravia Union, p. 3, Feb. 15, 1968.

"Pioneers spring big upset," San Francisco Examiner, p. F3, March 24, 1981.

"Polk girls drop to eighth," Corydon Times-Republican, p. 5, Dec. 27, 1973.

Pospisil, Stu. "George Nicodemus, 92, coached Husker women during lengthy career," omaha.com, Sept. 8, 2016.

Raffensperger, Gene. "Ex-disc jockey new Cornet owner," Des Moines Register, p. S1, Jan. 26, 1980.

"Ray's Ramblin's," Moravia Union, p. 2, Jan. 30, 1975.

"Rebounding costs Cornets' third loss, 115-106," Des Moines Tribune, p. 15, Dec. 28, 1979.

"Robin Tucker – Former Ohio State Women's Basketball Player," robin-tucker-ohio-state.blogspot.com.

Rosenthal, Bert. "'Machine Gun' back on track," Santa Fe New Mexican, p. 13, Dec. 3, 1982.

Roth, Evan. "A replay of Cornets' failure," Des Moines Tribune, p. 3, Aug. 28, 1982.

Runtagh, Jordan. "Studio 54: 10 Wild Stories From Club's Debauched Heyday," rollingstone.com, April 26, 2017.

"Scoring," imdb.com.

"Scoring," letterboxd.com.

Shranck, Bob. "Stopping Bolin key to Fillies' title hopes," Minneapolis Star, p. 10C, March 31, 1980.

Smith, Cindy. "Women's basketball league begins climb to credibility," The Tennessean, p. 17-C, Sept. 28, 1986.

"Viking women defeat Westmar," Des Moines Register, p. 30, Nov. 16, 1977.

"WBL vote is unanimous," Boston Globe, p. 26, Jan. 28, 1981.

"What If – Pete Maravich?" thomastontimes.com.

"Women's History Month: The WBL (1978-81)," aces.wnba.com, March 9, 2018.

About the author

    Stephen H. Provost is a lifelong sports fan who served as sports editor of two daily newspapers in California. He is the author of *A Whole Different League*, which chronicles the history of outlaw sports leagues. During more than three decades in journalism, he has worked as a managing editor, copy desk chief, columnist and reporter at five newspapers. Now a full-time author, he has written on such diverse topics as American highways, dragons, mutant superheroes, mythic archetypes, language, department stores and his hometown. He currently lives in Virginia. And he loves cats. Read his blogs and keep up with his activities at stephenhprovost.com.

Also by the author

Works of Fiction

The Memortality Saga

Memortality

Paralucidity

The Only Dragon

Identity Break

Feathercap

Nightmare's Eve

Works of Nonfiction

A Whole Different League

Highway 99

Fresno Growing Up

Undefeated

The Phoenix Chronicles

The Osiris Testament

The Way of the Phoenix

The Gospel of the Phoenix

The Phoenix Principle

Forged in Ancient Fires

Messiah in the Making

Requiem for a Phantom God

Media Meltdown in the Age of Trump

Please Stop Saying That!

Praise for other works

"The complex idea of mixing morality and mortality is a fresh twist on the human condition. ... **Memortality** is one of those books that will incite more questions than it answers. And for fandom, that's a good thing."

— Ricky L. Brown, Amazing Stories

"Punchy and fast paced, **Memortality** reads like a graphic novel. ... (Provost's) style makes the trippy landscapes and mind-bending plot points more believable and adds a thrilling edge to this vivid crossover fantasy."

— Foreword Reviews

"The genres in this volume span horror, fantasy, and science-fiction, and each is handled deftly. ... **Nightmare's Eve** should be on your reading list. The stories are at the intersection of nightmare and lucid dreaming, up ahead a signpost ... next stop, your reading pile. Keep the nightlight on."

— R.B. Payne, Cemetery Dance

"**Memortality** by Stephen Provost is a highly original, thrilling novel unlike anything else out there."

— David McAfee, bestselling author of 33 A.D., 61 A.D., and 79 A.D.

"Profusely illustrated throughout, **Highway 99** is unreservedly recommended as an essential and core addition to every community and academic library's California History collections."

— California Bookwatch

"As informed and informative as it is entertaining and absorbing, **Fresno Growing Up** is very highly recommended for personal, community, and academic library 20th Century American History collections."

— John Burroughs, Reviewer's Bookwatch

"Provost sticks mostly to the classics: vampires, ghosts, aliens, and even dragons. But trekking familiar terrain allows the author to subvert readers' expectations. ... Provost's poetry skillfully displays the same somber themes as the stories. ... Worthy tales that prove external forces are no more terrifying than what's inside people's heads."

— Kirkus Reviews on **Nightmare's Eve**

"… an engaging narrative that pulls the reader into the story and onto the road. ... I highly recommend **Highway 99: The History of California's Main Street**, whether you're a roadside archaeology nut or just someone who enjoys a ripping story peppered with vintage photographs."

— Barbara Gossett,
Society for Commercial Archaeology Journal

The Legend of Molly Bolin

33954349R00133

Made in the USA
San Bernardino, CA
28 April 2019